The Dalesman's
YORKSHIRE ANNUAL
1972

35p.

The Dalesman Publishing Company Ltd.,
Clapham (via Lancaster), Yorkshire

© The Dalesman Publishing Co. Ltd., 1971

ISBN: 0   85206   081   5

Printed and bound in Great Britain by
Galava Printing Co., Ltd., Hallam Road, Nelson, Lancs.

The Dalesman's
YORKSHIRE ANNUAL
1972

Dalesman Books

Contents

The cover painting of "The Swaledale Postman" is by Bernard Fearnley.

Uncredited drawings in the text are by Janet Acland, Stanley Bond and E. Gower.

Build your Castle on Skipton Foundations

foundations such as
constantly growing assets .With a
computer to watch them (not to mention
a Boardroom full of Yorkshire business-
men — to watch the computer !)
Why not build **your** castle on our solid
foundations ?

SKIPTON BUILDING SOCIETY

HEAD OFFICE: HIGH STREET, SKIPTON,
YORKSHIRE. TEL: 0756 - 2487 BD23 IDN

CITY OFFICE: 81 HIGH HOLBORN,
LONDON, WC1V 6NG TEL: 01 - 242 8147

Branches and Agencies throughout
the country

Member of the Building Societies Association (Trustee Status)

Growing and Growing

Introduction

THE onset of the 1970s saw "The Dalesman" well and truly past its coming-of-age and, in human terms, approaching its prime of life. This moment in our progress must have made us slightly light-headed, for last year we finally yielded to long-standing pressure from our readers and published the first "Yorkshire Annual." It was served up as "a feast of new reading by some of the best-known 'Dalesman' contributors." And the feast must have proved palatable, as we have had many requests for a second helping. Here it is.

Barrie Farnill, a noted authority on the Yorkshire Coast, writes on the halcyon days of smuggling in this area. Harry J. Scott, editor of "The Dalesman", asks, "Is there wit in Yorkshire's humour?" And William Hebden, author of "Yorkshire Battles," recounts the ill-fated Rising of the North and its associations with moated Markenfield Hall. Wild deer in Bowland are the subject of a contribution by W. R. Mitchell, while shepherds and sheep dogs form the centrepiece of an article by Edward Hart—farming correspondent of "The Dalesman." Guy Phillips takes an erudite look at the many mysterious rock formations in Yorkshire; "Quix" writes about the tragic railway accident at Ais Gill one wild night in 1913; and P. A. Burtt takes the reader on a tour of the highways and byways of Hambleton. We hope this is an annual which contains something for everyone.

Smuggling Days in Yorkshire

Barrie Farnill

IN the year 1849 the newly appointed coastguard officer at Robin Hood's Bay, near Whitby, Commander Richard Acheson, RN Retired, noticed that the most peculiar noises accompanied the spring tides—a clanking and thudding sound that seemed to spring from the bowels of the earth. Like all seamen, the good Commander was superstitious, but this did not scare him from his lawful occasions. Tales of "ghastlies and ghoulies" from the villagers had not deterred him from becoming the tenant of a house said to be haunted. The fact was that servants would not live in this house and came daily to perform their tasks.

But for the additional fact that occasionally a bulky parcel wrapped in sailcloth was found at the back door when it was unlocked in the mornings, the coastguard officer just might have been persuaded that no illicit cargoes were being landed on the coast nearby. But the parcels invariably contained a keg of brandy or a roll of Brussels lace. Each was turned over to the customs office.

Similar happenings had been taking place along the Yorkshire coast for well over 100 years. For the 18th century, and much of the following one, was the hey-day of the smuggling fraternity, with its highly organised gangs, ships and chain of distribution. Smuggling is a lot older than that and its practice, whatever the authorities say, is not ended yet. But in the days when this story is set, the smugglers were often violent as well as unlawful. Thus the Commander's wife declined to spent another night alone during a particularly noisy spring tide and he had to take her on patrol with him, muffled in a boat-cloak.

The officer thought he had made a thorough examination of all the caves in the neighbourhood. But after a few months he was inspecting

one narrow entrance when to his amazement he found a load of contraband. The smugglers were never caught, but the customs office made a fine example, and the psychological damage to the freetraders must have been enormous. But the story does not quite end there. Pushing past the kegs into the inner cave, the Commander discovered some recent masonry, and seizing a tool poked it vigorously to break through into his own front cellar. Or so it is said. This story was passed to me by the Commander's grand-daughter in the South of England. And it is a fact that many of the old buildings in and near The Dock at Robin Hood's Bay once connected with the old stream cavern which carries King's Beck to the sea.

This episode took place towards the end of the great smuggling days on the Yorkshire coast, when armed luggers and cutters sailed north-west from Flushing or some other Continental port almost nightly, prepared to race the Customs cutter and risk capture for the vast profits ensuing. By 1873 the Excisemen had a steam launch stationed at the Humber, and it was steam power which eventually played a big part in killing the smuggling trade. But before then, for 150 years and more, the freetraders raised mayhem.

A badly organised preventive system, short of ships and often enthusiasm, feebly tried to stem immense quantities of Dutch and French contraband. In 1784 there was only one revenue vessel at Hull, and two at Newcastle. Giant profits were made not only by the captains of the ships, and the syndicates of country farmers and yeomen who backed them, but by resident colonies of Englishmen living and trading in Holland. In 1746 probably 75 per cent of the tea consumed in England was smuggled. The drain on the national finances was great. The broad Humber estuary played a big part in the smuggling trade. Luggers would rendezvous with smaller craft from inland towns and transfer many nine gallon kegs of brandy, called ankers. One skipper made a profit of £250 on every shipment of 2,000 gallons in the early 18th century.

In 1732 Hornsea's parish clerk was also storekeeper to the local smuggling gang. He used the church's vaulted crypt as a storeroom, and one December night was counting stocks when a storm blew up. The steeple fell and the church roof was ripped off, so un-nerving the clerk that he was struck dumb. Probably a paralytic stroke was the reason but local pious folk affirmed that this was Heaven's judgment. Some time later one of the heads of the Hornsea gang was hanged in London and his body shipped home to hang on the gibbet as a warning to others.

Often a clever ruse would fox the customs men. At Bridlington a ship once arrived with her flag at half mast and the whole ship's company paraded behind six men bearing a coffin through the town. But the funeral never took place and soon a quantity of fine tobacco was on its way to York. Many were the dodges employed. False compartments, cavities of all kinds, and kegs with two compartments, one for some innocent substance in case of inspection, and the bottom one for brandy or Geneva (gin), were employed.

A favourite ploy was to drop a line of kegs roped together, with large stones to weight them down to the sea bottom, a little way offshore, so that local boats could creep out at low tide in darkness with grapnels. But the smugglers for many years disdained too much stealth, and risked their landings on the open shore at some village or cove where the excisemen could not reach them in time. It was a dangerous business often, not because of the customs vessels but because of informers who would alert the riding officers and soldiers who were stationed along the coast by the authorities.

Caves which riddle the Flamborough district were probably used. Robin Lyth's Hole, 50 feet high, is named after a legendary smuggler whom no bullet could harm. But these romantic figures are over-drawn. Of the character of the rough tough men, descendants of the Elizabethan seamen who did most of the smuggling, we can only guess. The penalties for smuggling were at times fierce. Heavy fines and long imprisonment were common. One notorious villain was fined a total of £100,000 in the mid-18th century. Luggers could be confiscated and broken up even on suspicion when they loitered within a few miles of the coast. Even landsmen who were found near the coast without reason could be whipped or jailed. Five years transportation was common for resisting the Customs men, while wounding an officer was punishable by death. But the rigorous laws were not always enforced. Often the smugglers were pressed into the Royal Navy and due to their excellent seamanship promotion to petty officer was common.

Famous smuggling inns were *The Ship Inn* at Saltburn; the *Old Mulgrave Castle Inn*, now no more; *The Ship Launch* at Whitby, now a cafe in Baxtergate, but with a smuggling ship figurehead outside its door; *The Old Fisherman's Arms* in Robin Hoods' Bay, now a private residence; *The Three Mariners* at Scarborough, for many years a museum; and *The Ship* at Filey, now also a private house. *The Ship Inn* at Saltburn was the headquarters of a famous smuggling gang led by John Andrew the licensee. A Scot, he ran the Cleveland Hunt for 50 years. He and a local brewer were partners and owned a fast and famous cutter, *The Morgan Rattler*. An underground

passage ran under *The Ship*, and the cellar under Andrew's nearby home, The White House, was only entered by a secret floor panel in the stable, over which was kept a mare celebrated for her spirited kicking. Eventually Andrew's greed gave him away. He was smuggling on such a large scale that capture was inevitable. Superintending a landing 20 miles from Saltburn in 1827, he was caught redhanded as the cargo beached, but he escaped and rode furiously to Hartlepool to try and establish an alibi. The attempt failed, he was imprisoned, could not pay a massive fine, and although released after a few years when influential friends had pleaded for him, never resumed his place as king of the north-east smugglers. He died in 1835.

Often furious sea-battles raged between the smugglers, who were frequently no better than pirates, and the excisemen. In 1777 the 200 ton schooner *Kent*, Dungeness-built as many of the smugglers

11

were, was captured in the North Sea by three frigates after an hour's continuous firing. Her captain, the notorious George Fagg, or "Stoney" was caught and five of her crew killed. She carried 8,000 gallons of spirit, and 500 bags of tea. In the early century off Robin Hood's Bay, which was the main rendezvous for smuggling vessels for many years, a battle took place between a revenue cutter and a lugger, and so many guns were firing it is said that one could read print by the flashes.

Often the local villagers were in league with the smugglers and this made detection and capture practically impossible. One insolent gang of Bay smugglers were said to have laid a trap for a customs vessel when a village informer rode to Scarborough to lay information against them. They awaited the cutter, not by their moored vessel but in another small boat, boarded the customs vessel after the officers took to their whaler to investigate the beach, and are said to have sailed it to Holland and sold it.

But although the big armed vessels frequently beat the government cutters off, the smaller ones were easier prey. In 1827 the tiny *Goede Hoop* of Ostend was captured off Whitby with gin, brandy, snuff, tobacco and tea in her hold. Its crew of eight Dutchmen were sent to York castle, each man unable to pay his £100 fine.

Land battles were frequent. In 1779 excisemen seized 200 casks of brandy and gin at Robin Hood's Bay, and the local men fought them to surrender. Another day in the village the officers actually caught the smugglers delivering into the cellars. On this celebrated occasion the officers decided to sample the goods from a leak in a cask and, according to tradition, the smugglers were able to return to the cellar and remove most of the contraband while the unwise law officers slumbered and snored in a drunken stupor.

Although many of the smugglers were professionals, the skippers of vessels otherwise engaged in lawful commerce did a tremendous amount also. Some collier captains returning to the Tees in ballast from the south of England would risk a quick trip to the Continent first. So well was distribution organised, even for the smaller men, that a typical "run" was that of a collier skipper who came into Stockton with 5,000 lb of tobacco. During the night it was transferred to a lighter and taken by river to Yarm, then brought by road to Sheffield and on to Chesterfield.

Romantic though the old days sound, the smugglers could be crude and violent. In the Cleveland area in the 1770s smuggling had reached such a peak, with armed gangs roaming the neighbourhood, setting fire to farms, slaughtering cattle and kidnapping women that the villagers were in constant fear of their lives and appealed for troops to be stationed in the area. In 1775 dragoons from York were placed on the coast in detachments. An NCO and 16 men went to Whitby.

Thirty years later the Whitby collector was still complaining to the Army commanders that Robin Hoods Bay and Staithes continued to be centres for big smuggling vessels, and that the local villagers were so in league with them that most of the contraband immediately disappeared from the beaches into the countryside. About this time it became obvious that many of the gentry were involved in the trade. One Sir Charles Turner was boasting, a scandalised customs officer wrote to his London headquarters, that he could get claret from Guernsey at the low price of 1s 6d per bottle, and offered to accommodate his friends at the same rate.

In the 1830s the dragoons were still stationed on the North Yorkshire coast, but this was really at the last of the great epoch. After the battle of Waterloo the Government could then devote its total naval strength to a coastal blockade, and over the next decade or two, because of this and the faster steam vessels used, smuggling was largely put down. That is not to say that it stopped. Or that has ever stopped altogether. Although the customs and excise detection system grew so efficiently over the years, it never managed to stop the odd individual venturing a "run."

Times have changed and so has the contraband. In the 18th and 19th century, spirits and tobacco, and at times tea, were the cargoes. Today occasionally in the newspapers you may read from time to time of some hapless seamen fined at a northern port for attempting to evade duty on various items. And not long since unsuccessful attempts were made to smuggle illegal immigrants into Yorkshire over the North Sea. One party actually evaded detection until they arrived in a big northern city. But today the amount of smuggling going on into the North is microscopic indeed compared with one of the most exciting eras in the history of the Yorkshire coast.

Yorkshire's "Pagan Rocks"

Guy Ragland Phillips
(with illustrations by the author)

CLIMB up the eastern side of Upper Nidderdale on to the moor strangely called Sype Land. There you will find two huge rocks which, once you have seen them, you will never forget. Around them are other rocks of fantastic shapes. Some of them invite comparison with altars, spinning-tops, or wild animals. But the scene as a whole is entirely dominated by the two colossi: Jenny Twigg and her Daughter Tib. These rocks and scars on Sype Land are examples of millstone grit eroded by natural forces, like the famous Brimham Rocks which are not many miles away. There is a difference, however. The surrounding rocks on Sype Land are mere scene-setters. It is Jenny Twigg and her Daughter Tib that inevitably occupy the centre of the stage. From some positions and in some climatic conditions— on a fine spring afternoon, for instance—they seem almost to be cavorting over the moor in a dream-world gavotte. At other times— twilight, say—they seem as you stand below them to be giants so old that they have long ceased to move, but not to live. At such moments they may be awe-inspiring.

Go now to Boroughbridge on the Great North Road. Just on the west side of the town stand three great pillars of millstone grit, evenly spaced and in a straight row from north to south. Erosion has been at work on these rocks, too. The rains of thousands of years have coursed down them, cutting them into deep parallel channels that reach from the top for two-thirds of the way to the ground level—below which lies much more of the rock. These three "Devil's Arrows" also cannot once be seen without being remembered ever after. They have the same sombre mystery and majesty that Jenny Twigg and her Daughter Tib embody. The Devil's Arrows were set up by men. It is believed that they were brought to

14

Wig Stones, Raygill Moor.

Boroughbridge (probably hauled on log rollers) from Plumpton Rocks, near Knaresborough—the nearest source of millstone grit. They must have been extremely important to warrant so great an effort. Their precise significance is unknown, but they can hardly have failed to serve a ceremonial and religious purpose. Perhaps the most interesting thing is that they were brought there and set up at all, in an area without rocks of its own. It suggests that where outstanding rocks were to be found naturally, these also might have been religious objects.

Archaeologists are at present compiling evidence about the pagan veneration of great natural rocks in Western Ireland, Wales and Brittany. Little has so far been done on those lines in England. "Jenny" is easily the name most commonly cited as that of alleged witches in the great trials of the 17th century. It was often handed down from mother to daughter along with the witchcraft (and handed down the name still is—in the same families). "Tib" is the name most usually given to a witch's "familiar," very often a black cat ("Tibby!"). But "Jenny" has connotations going back far beyond the witches. Near Gordale Scar is Jenny's Force, with a cave at the foot of the waterfall. In this cave, according to tradition, lived Jenny, who was no mere witch but "queen of the fairies in these parts." That is probably to say she was a local goddess. It is in "these parts", not so far away, that Jenny Twigg and her Daughter Tib stand.

Yorkshire is especially rich in strange rocks. Ilkley Moor, for instance, has many rocks which were carved thousands of years ago with the unexplained "cup-and-ring" markings and the enigmatic design of the Swastika Stone. It also has the natural Doubler Stones. Although there are two of these, it is by no means certain that the

15

name refers to that fact. It is locally pronounced "Doobler," although "double" is uttered as "dubble" in the ordinary way. At the opposite end of the moor is another great stack of cracked and broken grit with a huge flat cap-stone. This rock is very noticeable from the moor road below, and even from the main road running down the trough of Wharfedale. It is as natural as the Doublers, but it is known as the Idol Stone. The name may not be far from the truth. Relatively prosaic interpretations of topographical names were given, 50 years ago, partly in reaction against the romantic "Druidical" fantasies of last century. These apparently matter-of-fact versions, however, are now themselves being questioned.

The Wain Stones, on the North York Moors above Stokesley, used to be thought to have some reference to a hay-wain. It is now accepted that "Wain" means something like "sorrowing" or "sorrow-making." In two places on those same moors are man-made groups of rocks called "Bridestones." The late Frank Elgee, long before modern researchers in this field, pointed out the concurrence between

Devil's Arrow, Boroughbridge.

16

the northern group and certain astronomical phenomena. "Bride," however, almost certainly refers to a most ancient Celtic goddess who in Ireland was later canonised as St. Bridget. The name and the goddess may even go back beyond the Celts to the Bronze Age Iberians—and the Bridestones were established before ever the Celts arrived in Britain. If you stand within the group on a clear, starlit night, you will see what I mean, and you will not forget.

My own suspicions about names arose years ago. I was struck by the remarkable number of "rocking stones" indicated on the Ordnance Survey maps of the Yorkshire Dales. "Ah, well," I was told, "at the end of the Ice Age a lot of rocks were let down by the melting ice on to unstable resting-places." And I believed it. Then Mr. George Stoney, of Shipley, told me how he and a friend had once toured Yorkshire, systematically visiting every rocking-stone mapped. They completely failed to rock a single one of them.

Sir Kenneth Parkinson, looking at a picture entitled "Rocking Stone Hall," shook his head and told me: "That's not what the local people say. They call it Roggan Hall." The place is a shooting-box in two sections, with a great flat stone between them, on the summit of the moor between West End and Bolton Priory. The stone, he said, was called "Roggan Stone." If the building is known not as "Roggan Stone Hall" but simply "Roggan Hall," the implication is that "Roggan" is the name of the place and not a corruption of "rocking." In fact, I think that on the contrary "rocking stone" is a map-makers' corruption of "roggan stone." What that might mean I do not know. It must be admitted that the Anglo-Saxon for "to rock" is "roccian." The only trouble is that they do not rock. I have tried many of them myself, with no success.

Two other names which crop up on maps of the Yorkshire Dales are "Wig Stones" and "Hen Stones." There are two groups of "Wig Stones" on the moors to the west of Upper Nidderdale—the first between Ramsgill and the little-known mountain of Meugher, the other not far to the south above Grimwith. From Roggan Hall less than two miles north-west across the same moor is one group of "Hen Stones" (complete with another "rocking stone" that doesn't). A similar distance north of Roggan Hall is a second lot of "Hen Stones," and just east of Roggan Hall is a group of Raven Stones.

First, why Wig Stones? Because, you will be told, some of them look as if they are wearing wigs. And so indeed they do. But others do not, and still are Wig Stones. The academics explain that the word "wig" comes from a root which means "to rock." Here we are back again among the rockers, only now they wiggle. They don't do that, either. The letters "c" and "g" have a way of interchanging themselves philologically. And "wicca" is a witch or wizard. Perhaps here is where the explanation should be sought. At any rate, it might be said that the cap fits.

As for the Hen Stones, the name may refer to birds in general as it

Jenny Twig and her Daughter Tib, Sype Land, Nidderdale.

originally did, rather than to the female and rather than to poultry. Or it might be a Celtic word meaning "old." The first version is the more likely. If we are dealing with Bird Stones, we are back in the categories of mythology. Dr. Anne Ross has shown from many examples, including folklore, the religious importance of birds (with the raven prominent among them) for the Celts and indeed for all the ancient world. The Mórrígan, queen of the Irish gods, often assumed the shape of a bird, and was attended by a flock of birds which could be terrible in battle. In the Welsh myth, the birds of Rhiannon sang sweetly for seven years. Some of the groups of Hen Stones in Yorkshire are like the retinue of the Mórrígan. The row of bird-rocks north-west of Roggan Hall and visible from Simon's Seat have expressions of extreme ferocity and evil.

Simon's Seat, incidentally, is another of those millstone-grit names that are suspect. It is usually interpreted as meaning simply "the seat of Simon." But there is nothing whatever to indicate any Simon who might at some time have been sufficiently involved with Wharfedale to have a crag named after him. After all, Arthur's Seat at Edinburgh is now generally accepted as being really Airidh a-r' Sidh, the shieling of the elves. If the Yorkshire crag were Saimh an Sidh, that would be the sacred place of the elves.

When I first asked Nidderdale people what was the origin of the name Jenny Twigg and her Daughter Tib, I was told: "Probably

18

there was somebody of that name around here, with a daughter."
Maybe—but there is no record of any such person, let alone anybody
to be commemorated. The Ordnance Survey's authority for per-
petuating the name was destroyed in a blitz fire during the last war.
In any case, there they still stand, Jenny and Tib, lonely and magnificent, as commanding in their weird splendour as they were when they
were carved by unimaginable mills of wind and ice. They were there
when man first came to these parts. Those men could not conceivably
have ignored them. In the culture of such a society, the great rocks
must have formed a nucleus of human apprehension of the super-
human. It is difficult enough even today to stand before them
without a kind of humility, if only latent. Thousands of years ago, I
believe, they were gods.

Music
without distraction

Relatively small amounts of distortion can take the edge off the enjoyment of HI-FI sound, the result of this is often referred to as Listening Fatigue.

To be fair to all Customers who place a firm order for HI-FI, we offer and almost insist on a comprehensive listening test in the Home.

Although we have a Home Furnished HI-FI demonstration room at Settle, we know from experience that it will not "sound" the same as other rooms. It can in fact make a "strident" sounding Loudspeaker sound reasonable. The most important acoustic problem when choosing HI-FI is the customers Living/Listening room. Amplifiers also can produce a strident sound, which can be amplified or masked by room acoustics. These problems can only be ironed out by a Home listening test.

TERMS OF BUSINESS

Acoustic tests and installation using a Loudspeaker comparison switch in the customers home FREE, within a sixty-mile radius of Settle.

Twelve-month comprehensive guarantee at NO CHARGE.

Accounts are rendered NETT. WE cannot give these comprehensive tests and installations in the customers home FREE as well as a DISCOUNT.

We can arrange credit facilities to enable you to buy and enjoy the most modern HI-FI equipment, without disturbing your savings.

EQUIPMENT BY: QUAD, SONY, LEAK, TANDBERG, B. & O., CAMBRIDGE AUDIO, TRIO, SONAB.

SPEAKERS BY: QUAD, B. & O., B. & W., SONAB, MORDAUNT-SHORT, K.E.F., WHARFEDALE, and many others. Cabinets for HI-FI equipment by Record Housing, or we can arrange to fit the equipment in your own piece of furniture.

J. W. Garnett The HI-FI shop of the North West Settle 3558

A Corpulent Canon
of York . . .

The limerick—a form of verse well suited to Yorkshire humour— is enjoying a revival. These eight rhymes were submitted by "Dalesman" readers:

A corpulent Canon of York,
Religiously plied knife and fork.
He adored a York ham
And sometimes ate lamb,
But his principal passion was pork.

*   *   *

There was a young housewife of Pickering
Who marred married life by her bickering.
Her husband cried, "Jane,
Thy nattering's a bane.
And t'light o' my love's nobbut flickering!"

*   *   *

An unfortunate man up at Gayle
Dropped his teeth in the beck, says the tale,
Now a cow down at Hawes,
With the same size in jaws,
Has the prettiest smile in the Dale.

A miserly feller thra' Dent,
Run off, 'stead of payin' 'is rent.
　　Cried t' landlord—reight mad—
　　"Ah'll chase thee, my lad"—
An 'e did—'alf oop Penyghent!

*　　　*　　　*

There was an old farmer of Feizor
Who cut his wife's throat with a razor.
　　When they said, "Is that kind?"
　　He replied, "She doan't mind,
It nobbut tak's little to plaise 'er."

*　　　*　　　*

A tall lighthouse-keeper of Spurn
Saw the lighthouse collapse with concern;
　　But to full height he rose,
　　Hung the lamp on his nose,
And—there it continued to burn.

*　　　*　　　*

In winter an old girl of Reeth
Went around muffled up to the teeth:
　　To keep out the cold
　　She wore three skirts, I'm told,
And about seven woolly pairs underneath!

*　　　*　　　*

A short-sighted old lady of Wath
Was busily tasting her broth,
　　She tipped in the "Flit,"
　　Had a bit of a fit,
And flew out of the door as a moth.

Bowland's Whistling Deer

W. R. Mitchell

FOR the past four years I have studied the sika deer in Bowland, seeking them in all weathers: sunshine, rain, wind and snow. The most exciting period is autumn—the time of the whistling. When it is high summer, the sexes are segregated. Stags form small, all-male parties at the periphery of the range. During the day they lie up in the coolest, dampest parts of the woods to cheat the flies, and they emerge like shadows at dusk to feed on the protein-rich grasses of the meadows and rough grazings.

For weeks, their summer coats of dappled chestnut have contrasted strikingly with the lime green of grass in the shady deciduous woods. Then the thicker, darker—altogether drabber—winter coat begins to sprout through the summer pelage, being first revealed around the neck and upper parts of the body. Deer of temperate zones do not seem to hold their summer coat for long.

The summering stags grow new antlers to replace those cast in April. In three short months the horn growth is complete and by high summer their protective covering, a hairy skin called velvet, is shrivelling and falling away; the antlers can now be seen in their gleaming whiteness.

The hinds, or females, summer in the central areas of the range, and groups reform after the calving season. The pregnant hinds sought out secluded places like groves of holly and rhododendron where they might drop their young. As the season of the rut approaches, the coats of the hinds are still well-dappled but their calves are growing the drabber hair of the winter coat. Taking cover near the woods favoured by hinds, I have watched the parties emerge at last light to feed in "fog," which is the North Country term for the flush of sappy grass that follows the haytime mowing.

25

A Bowland stag in high summer (drawn by Margaret Hunter).

The rut is the period when the deer are sexually excited. Mammals exist primarily to propagate their kind, and creatures as socially-minded as deer have developed an elaborate ritual that leads up to the mating act. The ritual begins as the older, established stags invade the hinds' terrain. The stags seek out tracts of ground as territories, to be held against rival males, and meanwhile they claim the hinds that go with those tracts.

Phase One of the rutting season begins when a stag marks out its territory, drenching it with scent, which is the sikine equivalent of signs marked "Trespassers will be Prosecuted." By the end of September some of the Bowland woods are like Flanders battle-grounds. A stag marks the trees and ground at the edge of its territory by using its antlers like a flail, beating up whippy shrubs, threshing rhododendron; it also scythes the grasses.

The Flanders battlefield effect is created where the ground is marshy. A stag frenziedly churns up soft ground until a saucer-like, mud-filled depression has been created. Here the beast wallows, to emerge dark and dripping. The mud has the consistency of Yorkshire pudding mixture and retains marks of the stag's recent presence: prints of the feet, knees, antlers and even the pattern of hair on its back, each hair delicately impressed and the whole resembling lines on a fine etching.

The wallow, as used during the rut, is a means of transmitting scent, for when the stag has emerged from it the scent is soon spread on to foliage and vegetation via its antlers. I have seen stags simply lying in wallows, meanwhile rubbing their heads—and the scent glands of the head—against the ground and incidentally tossing sods and grasses. Stags look comical when wandering about at dusk with streamers of grass or thistles draped from their antlers. A wallowing stag exites other deer; sometimes I find a small wallow near a large one—a wallow doubtless made by a young stag that had been emulating the master.

When I go into the Bowland woods, my nose detects the general tang of deer. There are many subtle deer scents I cannot appreciate, yet a strange deer entering a territory will move through clouds of fine scent and read them as though they were a newspaper composed of vapour.

The whistling of the Bowland sika stag begins towards the end of September. Then the rut enters a second phase; it includes the mounting of the hinds as they come bleatingly into season. When I stand near a wood at the "edge o' dark," listening to the tawny owls going through their first round of territorial hooting, I sometimes hear the deer whistles at close quarters. The sound made by an amorous stag is not strictly a whistle. It is preceded by several deep grunts—*uh, uh, uh*. Then comes a high-pitched squeal, similar to the sound made by a pencil on an old-fashioned school slate. The sound is prolonged, gently rising and descending. There are usually three whistles in a sequence, and in the misty calm of the autumn night they are enchanting—like the piping of a northern Pan.

Is the whistling a proclamation of territory? Or is this strange autumnal call a means by which a stag attracts the hinds? The shrillest whistling in Bowland is made by some oldish stags in conifer forest at the head of the Hodder Valley. They go through the time-honoured ritual of the rut, and whistle very powerfully, in an area where hinds are rarely seen.

Outside the rut, a sikine whistle is short and sharp, uttered by both male and female, signifying alarm. The three evenly-spaced whistles of a stag in its territory are peculiar to the mating season, and so is a curious sound made by a stag in the near presence of hinds—sometimes, indeed, when there is a rival stag nearby. What begins as a clear whistle, rising smoothly in pitch, suddenly degenerates into an agonised groan. It has been heard in the reverse order, the groan coming first and the call developing into a whistle.

I have also heard a groan as of anguish, like a sound from prehis-

27

tory, invariably made by a stag near hinds. One October evening I watched a stag jog-trotting across a field near a conifer wood. It had been threshing the ground and lengths of bright green grass adorned the antlers. Some grass was draped over the stag's face, interfering with its vision, the stag jerked its head peevishly. The animal slowly moved back to the wood and stared among the trees for five minutes. From the wood emerged three hinds and a calf of the year; they began to graze quietly and the stag, standing about six yards from the nearest hind, held up its head and uttered a single, loud groaning. I am not yet certain of its significance.

I cannot predict just when a sikine whistle will be heard. The most likely times are dawn and dusk. At very close quarters the sound can be startling, sending a shiver up my spine, as though someone was tickling it with an icicle. A farmer walked through early morning mist, only 10 yards from an unseen stag, which began to call. The farmer felt his feet go cold; a chilling sensation advanced up his body to his scalp, and his hair seemed to stand on end. An old man suffering from arthritis of the leg joints was walking along a track between woods when a stag gave voice; the man ran for the first time in years and he also cleared a five-barred gate!

There is far more to the world of the deer than man can detect with his blunted senses. I went to the territory of a stag before dawn and listened to the animal through headphones attached to a tape recorder and parabolic reflector. The unseen stag was in an open field, and the beast grunted quite loudly for about five minutes before uttering each whistle. It seemed to spend most of its time grunting and snorting, and did this almost continuously for over an hour. Then dawn came and the animal went into the cover of the woods, but its loud whistling was heard when the morning was well advanced.

Stags are frequently heard about dusk. One evening, I was watching a stag grazing in a woodland glade when the whistling of two other stags, in different territories, reached me clearly. The stag I was watching did not react to the rivals' outcries. Even more interesting, especially during the night, is the opportunity of tracing the movements of an unseen stag by its whistling. A footloose stag will call as it moves around looking for hinds. A farmer was awakened by whistling at 4 a.m. and, listening to the sounds, he traced the movement of the stag up a deep gill and across a field. The last round of whistling occurred in the croft just outside the farmhouse.

Another special stag call I have heard during the rut is a goat-like bleating (a sound commonly made by hinds in season). I heard a male bleating during a battle between a master stag and the slightly younger animal that had the audacity to stand its ground when challenged. The master slowly advanced on the young stag, holding up its head in the threat display, which was ignored by the other.

The bleating sound came just before the first clatter of antler against antler. Then the battle—or, rather, a pushing match—began. The stags met head to head, with antlers crossed. A spirited fight raged for about a quarter of an hour, and although I stood only 15 yards away the stags ignored me totally. When the younger beast tired and lost its spirit, it ran off down a bracken-covered slope to a stream, splashed across and stood panting and steaming on the other bank, being too exhausted to move further. The master stag followed, standing in the stream with the peaty floodwater coursing around its sweat-matted legs.

After a quarter of an hour had passed, the stags recovered their strength and composure. The younger stag saw me and uttered a penetrating whistle (this time, the short and sharp whistle of alarm).

Who would expect to hear a shrill whistle from an animal as large and substantial as a deer? A Bowland farmer who had heard whistling from a local wood each autumn for many years thought that the sound was made by birds!

Pages from Yorkshire Artists' Sketchbooks

West End, drawn by Stanley Bond (opposite).

This hamlet in the upper Washburn Valley is now submerged beneath Leeds Corporation's Thruscross Reservoir. It was gradually abandoned over a long period, but the small church—in an exquisite setting of pine trees and mountain becks—remained to the end.

Muker, drawn by E. Jeffrey (page 32)

An upper Swaledale village with a population of under 500, and yet a parish covering 30,000 acres. The church was built in 1580; prior to this date coffins had to be taken down-dale to Grinton along the route of an ancient corpse way.

Warter, drawn by Ern Shaw (page 33)

An estate village in the heart of the Wolds, Warter stands on the site of an Augustinian priory founded over 800 years ago. The Warter estate was recently bought by a Guinness trust, the once famous gardens are no more.

Fylingthorpe, drawn by E. Gower (page 34)

This little-known community lies just to the west of Robin Hood's Bay. It has a number of interesting buildings and, like many of the villages in the surrounding area, boasts some keen quoits players.

Mid-Wharfedale, drawn by Janet Ellerington (page 35)

Although almost entirely part of the Chatsworth estate, this beautiful section of Wharfedale is readily accessible to the public. Features which have combined to make it a popular tourist area include Bolton Priory, the Strid and Barden Tower.

WEST END

Old Mill

The Church

·Stanley Bond·

Washburn Valley from East Gate

Muker

e. jeffrey

WARTER

TO Gt. DRIFFIELD
HUGGATE
NORTH DALTON
WARTER PRIORY
WARTER
MIDDLETON on the WOLDS
TO POCKLINGTON
TO BEVERLEY
To MARKET WEIGHTON

A row of Estate Cottages overlooking the village green - a masterpiece of the thatcher's art.

WARTER PRIORY

THE BOY WITH THE THORN after PRAXITELES

A FEW OF THE FEATURES IN THE FAMOUS GARDENS

THE WISHING WELL

WARTER CHURCH

Eron Shaw COPYRIGHT

The Yoke is still in use.

CAYTAN

"WINSTON" Note the walled up door.

THORPE HALL
TAUSYD
AD 1686

Peculiar house names:
IGDRASIL · LINGERS TOFT·
MINGO · MONGU·
all in
FYLING~
THORPE

Quoits are played
regularly. Each ring
weighs $5\frac{1}{4}$ lb

E.G.

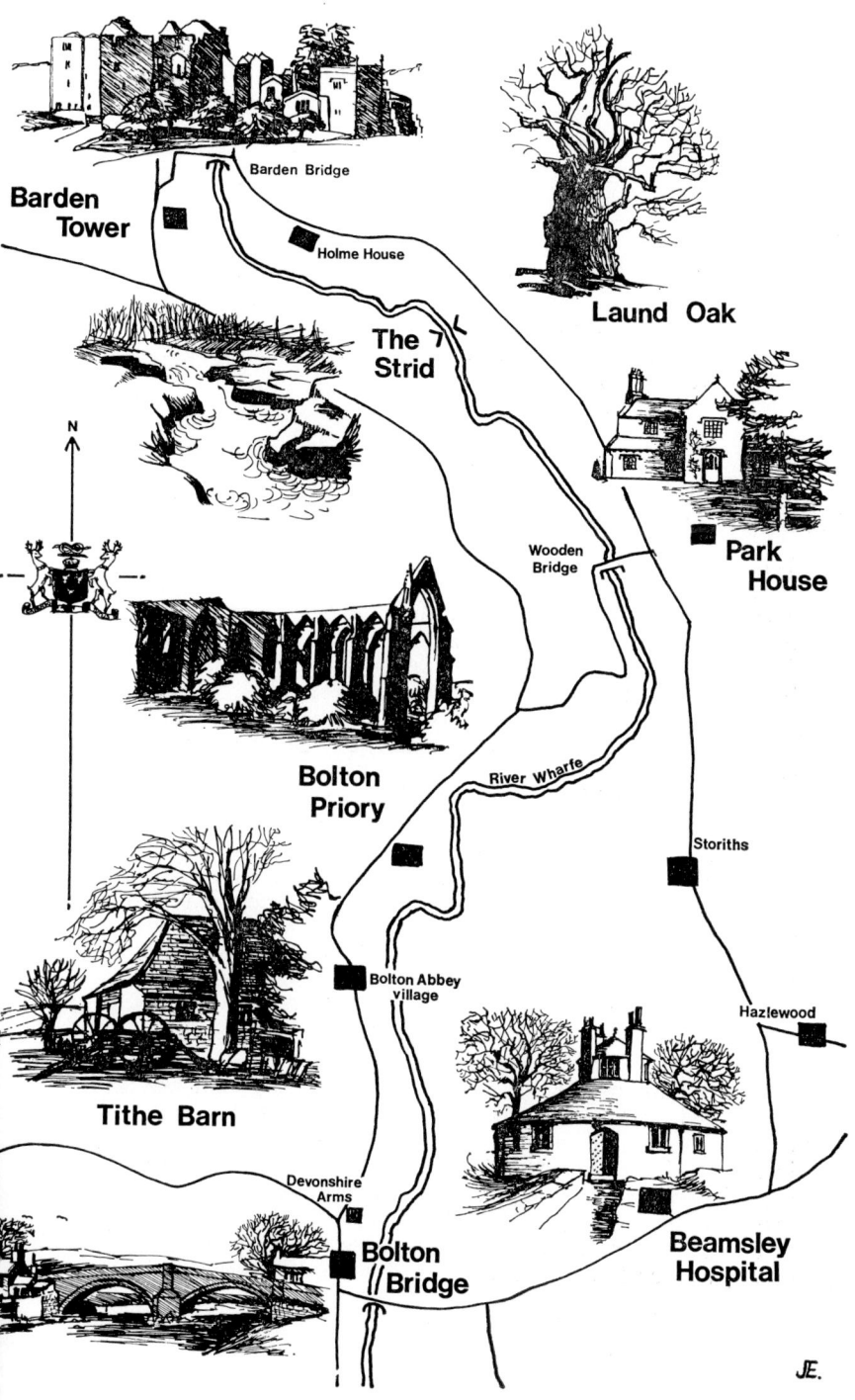

Barden Tower

Barden Bridge

Holme House

Laund Oak

The Strid

N

Wooden Bridge

Park House

Bolton Priory

River Wharfe

Storiths

Tithe Barn

Bolton Abbey village

Hazlewood

Devonshire Arms

Bolton Bridge

Beamsley Hospital

JE.

Disaster at Ais Gill

"Quix"

NO form of fast transport has a higher degree of safety than rail travel. That is why on those rare occasions when a major accident takes place the sense of dramatic tragedy is the more acute. At the same time there is often the feeling that the disaster resulted from trifling circumstances, or a marginal error which could have been avoided. No better instance can be recorded than that which occurred on a night almost sixty years ago. In the sequence of events human errors played their part, but the primary cause was a simple one, "Coal."

The Settle-Carlisle railroad crosses the wilds of the Pennines and its gradients and weather conditions make it a difficult route from the engine driver's point of view. Yet since the first passenger train used the line, some thirty-seven years went by with only one serious accident. The confidence of passengers was almost complete. Then came the early morning of the 2nd September 1913.

In the years just before the First World War, two night expresses left Carlisle soon after midnight for London. Train 993 hauled coaches from Stranraer and Glasgow. Train 446 was responsible for the Inverness and Edinburgh section, timed to depart fourteen minutes later. Train 993 received the green flag and moved out of Carlisle station on the first stage of its journey south. It was revealed afterwards that before leaving, the fireman had complained of indifferent coal, and that the driver was concerned at having a tare in excess of the maximum laid down for the long drag to Ais Gill summit. Whether or not there was any justification about the excessive load, there is no doubt whatsoever that a criticism of the coal was well founded. It was impossible to maintain a full head of steam, and as the gradient stiffened Train 993 was making heavy

Steam days on the Settle-Carlisle railway. The down "Thames-Clyde Express" between Blea Moor and Risehill tunnels, on the southern approach to Ais Gill summit (Eric Treacy).

weather of it. Both steam pressure and speed were falling steadily. By Intake Bank the speed of the train had dropped to less than 20 m.p.h. and, despite the driver giving his fireman what assistance he could, the train finally laboured to a halt within sight of Ais Gill summit, 1169 feet above sea level.

In accordance with correct railway practice, the guard descended from his van to find out the reason for the stoppage. "Short of steam," replied the driver, "we will be away in a minute." Accepting this assurance, the guard made no attempt to place detonators on the line. However, the signalman at Mallerstang retained his signals at danger and according to the book the stationary train was fully

37

protected.

Train No. 446 was making better progress and was picking up the minutes between the two trains. But the driver and fireman of this train also had their troubles. Water was low in the gauge due to a faulty injector, and in their efforts to remedy the defect they passed through the Mallerstang signals at red. The driver of Train No. 993, looking out from the cab of his stationary locomotive, saw the distant glare of a locomotive. So did the guard who, horror-stricken, rushed down the line waving his red lamp, while the driver tried hopelessly to get his train on the move. All was of no avail. The locomotive of Train 446 crashed into the rear coach of Train 993. This was in the days of gas lighting and the result was catastrophic. Fire broke out and within a minute escaping gas, fanned by the winds from the fells, turned the wreckage into an inferno. Near Ais Gill summit fourteen perished in the flames, and nearly three times that number were seriously injured on that early morning in September 1913.

Is there Wit in Yorkshire's Humour?

Harry J. Scott

A N odd thing happened the other evening. A gale which the B.B.C. had promised for days actually arrived and was sweeping through the streets in a wild fury. It appeared to have swept them clear of all but a few hardy pedestrians staggering rather than walking along. On the whole it was a grim, inhospitable evening and I was glad when I neared my friend Pottinger's house. That I knew would be a cheerful haven. I had reached the end of his road when suddenly I caught sight of a man's hat whisked high into the air and carried over a wall into a garden. Then I saw its owner, his hands clutching wildly at the place where his hat should have been. And I laughed out loud.

May I assume that you would have laughed too, for I want to establish at once my case that the sight of the man's hat blowing off in a gale is always an amusing sight, even though in cold logic you cannot say why. My friend Pottinger denies that, but I feel he was prejudiced for here is the oddity of the event—it was Pottinger's hat that I watched soar away, and it was Pottinger's hand I saw clutching at nothing! When Pottinger had recovered his hat and his temper we tried to reason this thing out in the warmth and comfort of his "den" while "the wind blew hard without"—as Shakespeare might have said.

Pottinger was quite blunt about it. He said I shared the York-shireman's crude mind, the sort that finds humour in other people's misfortunes, in schoolboy howlers, and in references by TV come-dians to mothers-in-law and kippers and Pudsey. I no doubt found delight in red noses and aspidistras and spring cleaning, and probably laughed myself sore at the mention of gorgonzola or tripe. I ad-mitted it all, but claimed that at least I had a sense of humour. For

41

NANCY METCALFE

Visitor: "What's that new building on the fell?"
Farmer: "If I can find a tenant, it's a bungalow; if I don't it's a barn."

example, I laughed the other day when I saw a benign gentleman motoring along a busy Leeds thoroughfare. Stopping at a red traffic light he caught sight of an elderly lady intent upon boarding a bus but confused by the traffic. Gallantly jumping from his car he hurried over and gently helped her on to the bus. Then he casually climbed on after her and sat down in the bus, leaving a traffic jam to pile up behind his car he'd absent-mindedly left at the lights.

"Isn't that humorous?" I asked.

"Like all Yorkshiremen", retorted Pottinger. "You confuse two things—humour and wit. Any fool can laugh at a joke, wit demands the response to intelligence. And that's where your sense of humour falls down."

It was a hard thrust and I wondered for a while if his diagnosis was correct. We are a dour, hard, undemonstrative people, inclined to take a matter-of-fact view of life, with little time to polish up subtle quips and jests. Dr. Phyllis Bentley tells the story of how she once walked on the hills above Halifax relaxing from a hard spell of writing. The sun shone, birds were singing, and there was a soft summer breeze to freshen the air. "Isn't this a wonderful day?"

42

"Ah've telled thee afore abaht standin' gossiping i' this sooart o' weather."

she said enthusiastically to a roadman as she passed.

"Aye, it's all right," he replied. "But there's no need to get into a lather about it."

That is one side of our Yorkshire character, probably most obvious to the outsider. We are frequently reminded of the Dales farmer who was given a "weather glass" to hang in his porch. Day after day he consulted it, but it stuck at "Set Fair" until in wrath he wrenched it off the wall and held it out in the rain. "Now then, see for thissen," he declared.

Yet we have a fund of traditional stories which have both humour and wit, like that of the farmer who met his farm lad going off work lone evening with an electric torch in his hand.

"Wheer's ta going wi' that thing?" he asked.

"Ah'm going courting," said the lad.

"Nay, Ah nivver took a torch when Ah went courting," remarked the farmer.

"Maybe, but see what tha picked up," retorted the lad.

We had a multitude of Yorkshire sayings which sum up a character

43

"He caught me using an electric
mixer for the Yorkshire Pudding."

or situation in a very few words, like that to describe a neighbour who is very well off: "He's that well off, he's bowlegged wi' brass." Or the response to the hiker who complained that it was a long lane to a certain farm: "Aye, but if it were any shorter it wouldn't reach." There was a Dales farmer I knew who, if he met me early in the morning, always declared: "You must have got up before you went anywhere." And his wife's favourite phrase was: "It doesn't take me long to do a five minute job."

Some of these quips may be generations old, but they remain coins, unlike some in modern currency, which never lose their brightness and rarely fail to bring a chuckle. Yet, as I reminded Mr. Pottinger, they are still being added to, as in the old dalesman's comment on the new decimal system: "Ah reckon t'pound won't go as far as it did—but it'll go faster." Perhaps it is the forthrightness of the Yorkshireman which hides much of the subtlety of his wit, like the old West Riding man who made a habit of attending funerals. He had attended the funerals of four of his pals or their wives within a few months. When a fifth went, his wife asked him why he wasn't going to that funeral. "Nay," he said, "Ah'd better stay at home. It looks bad to keep on accepting other folks' hospitality if tha's nowt o' t'sort of thi own to offer."

44

I doubt whether I fully convinced Pottinger, who was still vexed about his hat, for he began to evade the issue. I reminded him of an incident this summer in his own town when a cricket club secretary was in the pavilion when the telephone rang. Someone was inquiring for a member of the club who was not a particularly good player.

"Hold on", said the secretary. "He's just gone out to bat—but he'll be back in a moment."

"Wasn't that good Yorkshire wit?" I asked.

"He was probably a Lancashire man—that secretary," returned Pottinger, unfairly.

A Yorkshire Crossword

Compiled by S. C Hunter

ACROSS

1. Location of the Clevland Hills (5, 6).
7. First blew back in one across (7).
9. Lowest part of any drain? (5).
12. Hound sound following Robin Hood? (3).
14. Word in following clue, singularly enough! (7).
17. Is situated between the Cleveland Hills and Pennines (13).
19. Collect and compare with Talle Co? (7).
20. Follows the horn for E.R. resort (3).
22. And man this publication (5).
24. May be reached from Hull (7).
25. Cheese that can be obtained for the needy as well! (11).

DOWN

2. Town in W. R. on the River Wharfe (5).
3. It's fish for him! (3).
4. First citizen of Doncaster (3).
5. A physical reminder (5).
6. Mop up by giving directions to sailor (4).
8. Value Rix placed upon this abbey? (8).
10. . . . and must you tear forward to reach it for Fountains abbey? (5).
11. Is found between the Rivers Lune and Ribble (8).
13. Fuss indicated ahead of four down (3).
15. Before Antonio's head is found on the River Calder! (4).
16. He is always found in a cotton town (4).
17. Apparently sane Bedouin (5).
18. Glint from eleven down to make this single (3).
19. Valley of W.R. (5).
20. It's pretty tough in Sheffield (5).
21. Did they put the bite on Cleopatra as an afterthought? (4).
23. Message you'd be distressed to send (3).
24. Time for a bit of pageantry (3).

(*Solution on page* 75).

47

Christmas Present

Gordon Allen North

"I'M worried to death about dad," Madge said. She put down her knitting and looked across the hearth at Charlie.

Her husband sighed and lowered his evening paper. "What's he up to now?"

"I don't know, but, well, you know how careful he always is, never spending a penny if he can help it. Even saving out of his pension."

"Go on, love, let's hear the worst." Nothing Madge's father did ever surprised Charlie.

"That's just it. He's throwing his money about nowadays like a man with ten arms."

"I shall believe that when I see it." Charlie returned to his paper. "Maybe he hasn't got the hang of this new decimal currency yet, Madge. Anyway, who's been telling you all this?" he asked from behind the printed sheet.

"Mrs. Braithwaite, for one, and she usually knows what she's talking about. She says their Sam saw him in Smithson's the other day getting measured for a new suit. He paid a big deposit, too. And where do you think Mrs. Jackson saw him? In Featherglow's, the decorators, ordering them to paint the cottage. Ordering them, mind you, not simply asking for an estimate."

Charlie put down his paper. "Featherglow's? Why, they're the best firm in the district. That'll cost him a bob or two."

"And that isn't all, not by a long chalk. Oh, no." Madge wriggled uneasily in her chair. "I met Mr. Binns, the ironmonger, this morning, and what do you think he told me? He said that dad's had that perfectly good fireplace knocked out of the parlour and had a new one put in."

"And what was Binns after—the payment for it?"

"Oh, no, Charlie, he's been paid, but he said he thought he'd better mention it, especially as dad's considering a new sink unit for the scullery. I expect he wondered how far the old man could go. Well, you know, whether his credit was good. He told me that dad's ordered a new television set, a twenty-three inch one, *and* a new radio and . . ."

"Just a minute, Madge, just a minute, love, please." Charlie held up his hand. "Take your time, lass. I—I can hardly keep up with you. A twenty-three inch telly—and what?"

"A new radio, one of these VHF's, I think Mr. Binns called it, the very best, he said. You know, Charlie, I think Mr. Binns thinks that dad's, well, a bit, you know, a bit . . ." Madge stared helplessly across the hearth at the astonished face of her husband.

Charlie leaned forward in his chair. "And there's more than Mr. Binns thinks he's, well, you know, as you put it. What did I tell you after your mother died, Madge? Didn't I say the old boy would go crackers living up there all on his own?" Charlie saw the tears in his wife's eyes, and was quick to retract. "Oh, I didn't really mean it, Madge, you know that. There's nothing wrong with the old boy that way, rest assured. But what on earth can he be up to?" Charlie scratched his ear, a habit of his when puzzled. "When did you last see your dad, dear?"

Madge shook her head. "I'm not sure, but I think it would be about the first week in November. I feel a bit ashamed about not going up to see him lately, but, well, to tell you the truth, Charlie, I've been expecting him to pop in almost every day."

"It isn't like him not to call. I wonder if something's amiss. Maybe he's upset about something we've said to him." Charlie got to his feet. "I'll tell you what, Madge. I'll go up and see the old boy and find out."

Madge began to put away her knitting. "Shall I come with you, Charlie?"

"Oh, no, I shall be back inside the hour. Besides, if I don't hurry, I shall miss him. He'll be off to the club shortly." He looked at the clock. "I wonder what the old boy's up to?"

Madge's reply startled Charlie. "I—I think I know, dear."

"You think you know, Madge; what is it then? What is he up to?" The look of utter misery on Madge's face shook Charlie. He waited impatiently while his wife dabbed her eyes. "Well, dear?"

"It was something Mr. Binns said."

"Oh, damn Binns." Charlie's jaw stood out aggressively. "It strikes me that chap Binns has said a good deal more than he'd a right to say. Come on, Madge, out with it. What did Binns say?" Madge was busy with her handkerchief again, even sniffing a little, something most unusual for her, and her woebegone expression and drooping figure disturbed Charlie. He began to wonder whether he should not perhaps have a private word with Binns, and ask the ironmonger to keep his business transactions to himself. Come to think of it, Binns *was* a bit of a scaremonger. Still, that could wait. Charlie smiled encouragingly at his wife. "You were saying, darling?"

"I—I think dad's expecting us to—to foot the bill for all this as—a—as a—" Madge burst into tears. "Oh, dear, Charlie, whatever are we going to do?"

"As a what, love? Come on, dear," Charlie prompted.

"As a—as a Christmas present." Madge dabbed her eyes.

Charlie straightened up as if a rod had been pushed against his spine. His chin came to the fore again. He stared unbelievingly at his wife. For a moment he had difficulty in speaking, but for only a moment, and then the words tumbled out. "As a Christmas present? Us? All that lot? Why, the old boy must have gone completely off his rocker."

"That's what Mr. Binns said he said—a Christmas present from you and me. 'Our Madge and Charlie,' he said."

"Where's my coat and hat? I'd better be on my way, Madge."

Charlie dragged on his coat while Madge stood holding his hat. "You're sure you don't want me to go with you, Charlie. You know how stubborn father can be when he feels that way."

"You get on with your knitting, lass. I think this is something that's best left to me." He jammed on his hat. "Let's see," he said. "I must get the details right. I want to know what I'm talking about up yonder." He began itemising on his fingers. "A new suit, for a start. Then the painting of the cottage. A twenty-three inch telly; a radio—and—what else, Madge? I'm sure there was something else.

51

What was it, Madge?"

"A new sink unit."

"That's it, a new sink unit. That's a laugh, anyway. What does he want with a new sink unit? He uses the same pot and plate, the same knife and fork and spoon over and over again, if I remember rightly. You can wash up in two minutes dead up yonder any old day, yes, and have everything back in the cupboard, all spick and span."

"Nay, I'm not having that, Charlie. Dad likes a good meal every now and then—like anybody else."

"I know that, love; you've no need to tell me that; and where does he get them? Either here or at your Mary Ellen's. I know. Sometimes at your Jack's when he's a bit hard pushed."

"That's not fair, Charlie, and you know it. Dad isn't all that bad. Why, I've seen the day when . . ."

Charlie held up his hand for silence. "I'd better be on my way, love," he said. As he reached the door, he turned and looked back at Madge. "I say, Madge, your dad doesn't know about the deposit we've saved for a house, does he?"

Madge nodded. "I mentioned it to him a few weeks ago."

The old man's cottage stood alone on a steep Pennine slope a mile away. Even in the dark Charlie could see that the cottage was newly painted. His heart sank at the sight of a new, elaborately-carved signboard standing at the side of the white gate. His mind was assessing the cost of the sign as he knocked hard on the cottage door. He had to knock again before the old man, puffing freely at a large meerchaum pipe, opened the door. An aroma of expensive tobacco surrounded Charlie. "Oh, it's you, Charlie. I wondered whoever it could be at this time of the evening. Come in, lad, come in."

Charlie saw the new fireplace at once. There was no twenty-three inch telly yet, thank goodness. But there was new wall-lighting, and new carpets, and, good heavens, whatever was the old boy wearing? Charlie stared unbelievingly at the crimson velvet smoking jacket adorning the upper half of his father-in-law. The jacket was so new that the gold facings glinted in the firelight. The old man waved a friendly arm in the direction of a chair. "Sit down, Charlie, boy," he invited. Charlie saw that the chair was a new one; it was an expensive make. Charlie vaguely remembered the price tag he had seen attached to a similar chair in the window of a shop in the valley town. The thought disturbed him. He did not sit down. Instead, he pulled his old working overcoat more closely about him as he stepped gingerly on to the new rug in front of the fireplace.

"Nay, I'll stand, thanks. I've only popped in for a minute or two." He looked hard at the old man. "I—er—I see you've had a new fireplace put in."

"Yes, do you like it, Charlie?" The old man stood back and surveyed the fireplace with the eye of a connoisseur inspecting a masterpiece. "Quite reasonable it was, too, and, well, just right for the cottage, don't you think?"

It was exactly right, Charlie thought, and so, too, was everything else in the place. The old boy had good taste, you could say that for him. Charlie knew that he would have been delighted with everything he had seen in the cottage—if it had not been for the gnawing ache at the very pit of his stomach. What, in the name of all that was sensible, had it all cost? And who was going to foot the bill? Was

the old man stark, raving bonkers? He nodded at the fireplace. "It's all right; just the ticket," he said.

"I'm glad you like it, Charlie. Here, what about a pipe of tobacco? Have you your pipe with you?" The old man whipped the lid off a tobacco bowl that Charlie had not seen before. The agreeable fragrance of expensive tobacco which filled Charlie's nostrils caused him to lean forward enthusiastically and sniff appreciatively at the contents of the almost full jar. He was groping happily for his pipe when the thought of the cost of the tobacco struck him like a punch in the solar plexus. The old man was holding the jar to his own nose and sniffing at its contents. "I always said I should smoke nothing but the best if I ever got the chance," he smiled. "This is the real stuff, Charlie, boy, the real stuff." He pushed the bowl in Charlie's direction.

Charlie shook his head. "Some other day, Pop. I—I really haven't the time tonight."

"I understand, Charlie." The old man nodded sympathetically. He replaced the bowl on the sideboard. "I know just how you feel, Charlie. You want your feet up to enjoy the full flavour of the best.

53

Yes, and all the time in the world to do it in, too." He indicated a chair. "I wish you'd sit down, lad, you can't be as pushed for time as all that."

Charlie ignored the invitation. "You've been painting the place," he said.

"Oh, the outside, you mean. Nay, I didn't do it myself. I've had Featherglow's up. A couple of chaps were at it for the best part of a week."

"They—er—they'd charge you a bob or two, I reckon, would Featherglow's? I mean, well, they're a first-class firm, aren't they?"

"The best in the valley, bar none, lad. They're a bit expensive, mind you, but I wanted a good job done, and they've done one. It's a pity it's dark, or you could have seen for yourself. I can recommend 'em. By the way, did you notice the new sign I've had put up, near the gate? Wrought iron and real English oak, they tell me. I picked it out of a catalogue. I wondered whatever I was going to get, but it turned out all right. Pretty costly, though."

Charlie felt too weak for comment. He nodded, and managed to croak: "Yes, I saw it as I came in at the gate." He tried to smile. "It—er—it looked very nice," he added. He looked searchingly at the old man. There was nothing strange about him as far as Charlie could see; he talked rationally enough and there was nothing peculiar in his actions. He was, perhaps, a little over-enthusiastic about his new possessions, but then, who wouldn't be? The place was a joy to see. The old man had settled down in an easy chair near his bookshelves. He had crossed his legs, and was puffing comfortably

at his pipe. He was a great reader. Charlie noticed that the upper shelves of the bookcase were stacked with new books. The splash of colour looked like a modern painting. Charlie's eyes roved round the room. There was a new clock on the sideboard that must have set the old man back a pound or two. And wasn't that a new electric-shaver in the half-opened package beside the clock? His eyes came to rest on his father-in-law.

The old man smiled at him. "Well, what do you think, Charlie? Do you like the place?" Charlie nodded. He could not trust himself to speak. The old man looked lovingly round the room. Then he waved an encompassing arm. "Thanks to you and Madge," he said.

Charles sank on to a chair. The old man rattled on. "I had a word with Binns the other day about a new sink unit for the scullery, but I thought I'd see what Madge had to say before I made up my mind about one. Oh, and I'm going in for a new telly, one with a bigger screen. I'd wondered about a twenty-three inch model. What do you think, Charlie?"

"Did I—did I hear you say 'thanks to you and Madge?' " Charlie asked. The sweat stood out in tiny globules on his forehead. He was aware that his mouth had fallen open as he stared, as if transfixed, at the round, plump, comfortable face of the old man.

The old man's eyes twinkled. "You did, Charlie, you did, lad. Your Christmas present, you know. Have you forgotten?"

"For—forgotten?" Charlie nearly choked. "Our—our Christmas present?"

"Yes, of course." The old man smiled benignly at his son-in-law. "The premium bond that you and Madge bought me for Christmas last year, remember? It came up in the November draw. Five-hundred pounds. Well, as I'm not without a bob or two for a rainy day, I thought I'd spend the money."

Sheep and Shepherds

Edward Hart

PICTURE a shepherd on a winter's night after his round on the hill. Visualise him before a glowing fire, with dogs stretched out lazily on the mat, and a selection of shepherds' crooks hung on the wall. Add a pair of boots drying, and you have really encompassed all necessities for a shepherd. He may have hypodermic syringe or drenching gun rinsing in a pan, but basically his tools and equipment are the same as they have been since man first began to shepherd the uplands of Yorkshire.

The shepherd's remains a very self-sufficient life. His stock graze outside summer and winter alike, consuming the natural herbage supplemented by hay cut from the few precious in-bye fields. Sugar beet pulp nuts or compound cake may be bought around lambing time, but do not alter fundamentals. The only literature really necessary is the Shepherds' Guide containing all the various earmarks used in the neighbourhood, and a Flock Book recording pedigrees. Even the fire may have changed little since the days when the cottage first withstood winter storms. Peat is still used for fuel, though not so commonly as in former times. Better roads mean access for coal wagons or even oil tankers, but peat has one indisputable advantage—it is free for cutting.

Peat harvest begins when lambing time closes. In fact, the lambing man hired on some large farms may be asked to stay an extra week to help with the peats. Late May is usual time for a start, the site being alongside a previous trench. First step is removal of the top sod. A long handled spade is used for this, and the cut turves are placed neatly on the peat bottom bared in last year's work. At one time the worth of a new hired shepherd was judged by the way he set his turves!

A characteristic Dales scene, with sheep and lambs being shepherded along a narrow country road (Cyril Harrington).

Cutting the peat proper now begins. The peat knife has a long blade like a hay spade, with a right-angled lug to give vertical as well as horizontal cut. It is thrust deep into the peat alongside the trench cut last year. It may be two, three, or four cuts wide. In front of the cutter stands the "flinger-out." His job is to take each slice of peat as it is cut, and fling it on to the grass alongside. A careful man, the flinger-out; if he allows his attention to be diverted by the call of the lark overhead, or the bleat of a black-faced lamb, he is in danger of losing a finger. He grips each peat after the cutter has thrust, lifted his blade, and made that slight forwards movement which liberates the peat from its base. Before the operation starts, it may be advisable to burn the herbage on which peats will be laid, to give level surface. Flinging-out is no more haphazard a process than is anything else in farming. The peats must touch each other, to prevent grass growing up between them. They must be angled slightly backwards from the thrower, allowing him room to work as the peats fall thick and fast.

And they must be thrown flat, and not broken by clumsy hands.

On a warm spring evening, the task is pleasant enough. On a cold one, when northerly blasts feel as though they have come non-stop from the Arctic to whistle round Tan Hill, there is strong temptation to call it a day and ring the coalman. Dank, wet peats can be unbelievably cold after a few score of them have been handled. If one is lucky with the weather, peat harvest brings memories of summer which last until the turves are glowing on a February night. It is very pleasant then to think of the June evening when a red-streaked sky flushed against distant hills, when the clean, sweet air of the uplands brought hearty appetite, and the only sounds were of curlew and ewe calling lamb. A peat fire recalls the essence of late spring, just as a handful of hay pulled at arm's length from a dales stack recaptures the essence of high summer.

A skilled cutter cleaves each peat exactly the same. With the inexperienced, slim ones—"real ladies' peats"—or long and fat ones —"Saturday nighters"—crop up among the rest. Saturday was the night when even the hardest working shepherd had an extra fireside spell. After the peats have dried for ten days or a fortnight, they are "fitted." This term describes the practice of fitting one against the other in inverted "V" formation, with the undersides placed outwards. A further spell of drying brings on the time for heaping, or reckling as it may be termed. These piles are the equivalent of the hay cock or pike. The base of the heap is built carefully to allow air to circulate, while on top the peats are placed crosswise, but still roughly so as to let upland breezes do their best. At this stage there is some protection against heavy rain, but also chance for the peats to dry further before stacking.

Final stage is leading by tractor and trailer into a neat, cottage-side stack, or under a building. The old standard was one cartload per week. Some modern combustion stoves function well enough on peat, heating the whole house against the worst that a northern hill winter can do. In a surprisingly short time, each peat has changed from a black, soggy, buttery slice into a solid but light rectangle with corners sharp enough to skin the fingers. Whether in Ireland, north of the Border or in a Yorkshire dales farmhouse, they burn with the golden glow that warms the heart as well as the body.

In front of the shepherd's peat fire, his dogs lie luxuriously, recuperating from a strenuous day in which they have covered many more miles than their master, who may have ten or a score to his credit. They may be kennelled outside, and only a faithful old pensioner allowed the privilege of the fireside. Wherever they are, we hope that they are dry and well cared for, and not worked to their limits simply because of their love of the job. It will not be long before the shepherd speaks of his dogs. Other professionals may talk of holidays, last week's dining-out evening, a television show or something equally fatuous, but your true hill shepherd is more

Portrait of a sheepdog—alert eyes and twitching nose (Bertram Unne).

interested in his charges than in anything else in the world.

The breeding of each dog will be known. "This black-and-white bitch is Bathgate Rock-bred; the similarly marked dog outside is a Wiston Capper, while here is a young one in pup to Llyr Evans' Bosworth Coon." Talk on breeding soon raises arguments among any class of stockmen, and certainly not least among sheep farmers. Yorkshire has its quota of notable dog handlers, and the Holmes brothers of Ripponden, Halifax, have been to the fore for many years. John Holliday has captained the English team, leaving his pleasant Pateley Bridge home to compete against the best with dogs like Moss and Glen. From the lowlands near Hovingham, Mr. and Mrs. Alan Heaton of Peel Park are both keen judges.

A regular circuit of sheep dog trials now takes place on most Saturdays, culminating in the Nationals and the International, which is to be staged at Newcastle-upon-Tyne in 1972. There are also various inter-club competitions, some encouraging keen Yorkshire/Lancashire rivalry. Several top handlers live just beyond the Broadacres boundary, including the Longton brothers, Tim and Tot. Cap and Ken, Rob and Nip were among the best known dogs in brace championships a few years ago, but now only Rob remains in competitions. This grand old collie, now ten years old, was retired by Tot Longton early in 1971. Rob thought otherwise. He refused to settle to a non-competitive old age, and re-emerged one rather foul day in the Scottish Borders as the only collie to master some very wilful sheep. He left the field to spontaneous applause from the gathering of shepherds, not usually the most demonstrative of men.

Another Lancastrian, Jim Cropper, with Fleet, Vic and Clyde, is a regular competitor, and was youngest entrant at the 1970 International at Kilmartin, among Argyll's towering mountains. Len Greenwood, now a septuagenarian, has had a string of good dogs for years, and now runs Sweep. No matter how keen the trial field atmosphere, the practical side is never overlooked. Hill sheep farming without good dogs would be quite impossible, and the sight of a large flock being gathered on a steep mountain side by a team of highly trained, intelligent dogs is one that never loses its appeal.

Almost as indispensable as the dog is the shepherd's crook, his "third leg" when walking up a winding trod, his "third arm" when extended to bring a flying hill ewe to book in a single movement. Stick making is as old as shepherding itself. The hotbed of this ancient craft is Northumberland and the Scottish Borders, but Yorkshire stick dressers acquit themselves very well. Mr. Frank Graham, formerly at Grimesgill, Masham, has now moved to an adjacent holding nearer the road, and is a keen fashioner of wood and horn. Some of his carvings are a delight to the eye, and are eagerly sought after by those who have patience to wait for what is a sideline in a busy farming life. Cow, deer, and goat horn have been carved by skilful hands into stick heads and ornaments, the more precious for having no counterpart in this mass-production age.

Many a good stick was carved in the shepherds' cottages first mentioned in discussing peat fires. The rather meagre light of a lantern was not good for reading, but sufficient to work away at the hours of "elbow grease" that go into stick making. A further advantage was that heat from the lamp could be used for bending the horn. Crooks are of two main types, a neck crook and a leg crook. The latter has a much smaller mouth, to which it is long in proportion, and the sheep is hooked by a hind leg. Walking sticks are of various types: thumb sticks are a Yorkshire speciality, while also made are gamekeepers' sticks with heavy knobs, and sticks with wood or horn handles according to the fist of the user.

One charm of sticks is their endless variety. Hazel is deservedly popular, for even in this one species are many types. Bark may be thick or thin, dark, light, or mottled. The skilled stick maker brings out natural beauty in a shank; he does not try to fit all into a common mold. Hazel is readily available in Yorkshire, though extensive coniferous plantings are no more beneficial to it than they are to anything else. The head may be in one piece with the shank, in which case a straight shank is chosen. A block of wood from the branch from which it springs is then sawn off to be shaped into the head. If wood heads are joined to the shank by means of a peg, the hardest timber from which to fashion them is from those rounded lumps which appear on old elm trunks. Ash, blackthorn, holly and a form of willow are all useful.

Horns are more of a limiting factor. A Blackface, Lonk, Swaledale or Dalesbred tup may have formidable horns, but they tend to be damaged as old age approaches. No two horns are alike, and none is perfect. The stick maker must work with material to hand, and make the best of it, as he does of dales weather whatever the season.

"Then you pen 'em like this—see?"

Rebellion at Markenfield

William Hebden

THE time-encrusted mansion of Markenfield Hall, near Ripon, was deeply involved in one of the most terrible armed rebellions that ever shook the north. Built by John de Markenfield, a former Chancellor of England, about the year 1310 and listed as a fortified manor house in the reign of Elizabeth the First, no more suitable background could be discovered in Britain for the steel-corseleted hosts of bygone wars. To take the road from Ripley to Ripon and, half a mile beyond the Bishop Monkton and Fountains Abbey crossroads, to make one's way—opening and shutting two gates— by way of the long farm road, is to stumble on a scene unchanged through centuries. The same grey bridge, once a drawbridge, the deep, silent moat—for Markenfield is one of the few moated manor houses in England—the tall minarets, the battlements and vast empty rooms, are only matched by the enormous half-grassed, half-cobbled courtyard.

From here rode Yorkshire contingents to Agincourt, Flodden and then—that last great gesture of Markenfield—the Rising of the North. The year 1536, some thirty years previous to the above rebellion, had witnessed the closure by King Henry the Eighth of many monasteries including Fountains Abbey. Immediately following these closures, the angry uprising known as the Pilgrimage of Grace had been crushed by the King with terrible ferocity. For many years following this rebellion, the hate of the northern Catholics for the jumped up "southrons" who, under one pretext or another, had snatched the abbey lands, had smouldered like a moor fire. Now, in 1569 it burst into sudden flame.

The rebellion was led around Ripon by Thomas Markenfield, long self-exiled abroad on account of his faith. To Markenfield Hall

Markenfield Hall is one of the most perfect examples of a medieval manor house. Built in the 14th century and surrounded by a moat, it is entered by a fine Tudor gatehouse. A bridge has taken the place of the drawbridge, and to step across it into the courtyard is like stepping into a by-gone age.

Stanley Bond.

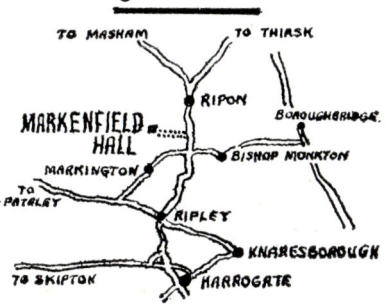

TO MASHAM — TO THIRSK

RIPON

MARKENFIELD HALL

BOROUGHBRIDGE

MARKINGTON

BISHOP MONKTON

TO PATELEY

RIPLEY

TO SKIPTON

KNARESBOROUGH

HARROGATE

there rode by night Dr Nicholas Morton, a dispossessed prebendary of York, bringing news that a great uprising on behalf of Mary Queen of Scots was being planned against Elizabeth the Queen. Immediately on hearing this news, Markenfield rode across country to Norton Conyers near Ripon and to Rilston Castle, "nigh the dale of Wharfe," and enlisted the willing help of the Yorkshire family of Norton. Headed by Richard Norton, High Sheriff of York, which made the rebellion of even greater portent, the proposed rising was sponsored by most of Norton's elder sons, only the three younger remaining loyal to the Queen.

Much has been written of the Rebellion of the North in which were involved not only Markenfield and the Nortons but the great houses of Percy and Neville, Earls of Northumberland and West-moreland, together with many Ripon and North Yorkshire families of less account. Of the meeting of the rebels at Markenfield Hall and later at Topcliffe—where the Percy manor house may still be traced—the records of the north abound. From Topcliffe, the rebels journeyed to Brancepeth Castle on the Durham border, marched into Durham

63

The courtyard of Markenfield Hall, as seen through the gatehouse. This historic building is open to the public on Mondays from May to September.

Cathedral and, after burning the established prayer book there, came marching southwards via Richmond, Darlington and North-allerton to Ripon and Markenfield.

Standing today in Markenfield's courtyard, one may readily imagine the great and colourful scene with the rebels parading beneath the Norton banner, "God us Ayde." They took the sacrament in Ripon Minster and then the London road, but got only as far as Doncaster. Had the rebellion been properly organised it might well have mastered England, but the entire plot was betrayed by its own leaders. Faced by the royal troops, the rebellion ended in a welter of broken hopes. Old Norton and young Markenfield fled abroad and most of the "eight goode sonnes" of the former were dispossessed or executed in London. The great Earls made for the heather and the Queen's troops were everywhere. Hundreds of ordinary people, strung upon gallows between Ripon and Darlington, left their names to be traced by the genealogist of today

As for the Markenfields, who throughout so many centuries had tilled their lands, walked their pleasaunces, finally to be carried in burial to Fountains or to their great burial vault in Ripon Minster, their name has faded from the land. In 1632 there still remained a few of their name—in Thomas Markenfield, a lawyer of Lincoln's Inn; in William Markenfield, Gent, of Markington; and in Henry Markenfield, "surgeon barber" of Ripon city. As for the Nortons, their castle of Rilston was torn to the ground and their lovely manor house of Norton Conyers passed into other hands. One is glad to hear of their becoming great again—in the person of Fletcher Norton, descended from the loyal son, Edmund. As Chief Justice of the Common Pleas and Speaker of the House of Commons, he was raised in 1769 to the peerage as first Baron Grantley. In purchasing the great house itself, he added to his title the name of Markenfield. Wandering around the old house today, one feels grateful to the present owner, Lord Grantley of Markenfield, in adding this splendid old fortress to the "open" mansions of England.

Battle at Towton Field

How like all other country fields
These meadow acres lie content;
To eye and ear and sense they yield
Bird's flight and song and honeyed scent;
But wait and you will feel the thud,
The solemn dreadful march of those
Who come to shed their English blood
In quarrels stemming from a rose;
In stillness you will hear the cries
Of horror, rage and ghastly strife
And lonely, dying, breathing sighs
As strong and gentle men lose life;
Go then to York and kneeling there
Remember in that shrine of prayer
Those stones looked down on Towton lads
Before war's fury drove them mad;
Then rise, give thanks those days are gone
When brothers fought and cold death won.

—S. L. Henderson Smith

Eye for the Dales

Janet Rawlins

JANET RAWLINS has a unique vision of the Yorkshire Dales. She interprets the area as a region of stark shapes, with rugged and imposing rocks, dry-stone walls and vernacular buildings. Wind-blown trees act as a foil to gaunt-looking houses or are themselves dominated by water-torn limestone gorges. It is a realistic portrayal. Artists have so often over-glamourised the Dales, depicting a soft and pastoral landscape or representing a countryside that seems to be baked by everlasting Mediterranean sun.

It was as a book illustrator and teacher that Janet Rawlins trained at Leeds College of Art. In her work as a freelance artist she has designed interiors, textiles, toys, inn signs and greetings cards, and has had exhibitions of her paintings and fabric collages in many northern galleries.

Opposite, top: Loup Scar, a limestone gorge on the river Wharfe just north of Burnsall.
Opposite, bottom: White Wells, a dominant landmark on the crest of Ilkley Moor.

Above: Dry-stone walls at Sedbusk, Wensleydale.

Opposite, top: In a Dales cottage.

Opposite bottom: Quiet corner at Draughton, near Skipton.

Top: Malham village.
Bottom: Wensleydale landscape.

70

Fine
Bone China and
Hand Cut Crystal.
   An investment in
Beauty–holds a value
and status Aesthetic and
Practical.
   To Give–Collect–or Receive.
Dependable Quality in a Plastic
World.

Hambleton Highways and Byways

P. A. Burtt

HIGH up on Hambleton is one of Yorkshire's great highways—the greatest perhaps in the literal sense of the word—for here we have only the sky above us, and we gaze down over vast distances, over the great plain of York to the western dales and Pennines beyond. Travelling eastwards over the broad acres, we have left behind the grey limestone country with its undulating pasture land and dry stone walls, passed through villages and hamlets with their stone-slated houses, and then almost unconsciously we are aware of a change in the general pattern of the countryside—the land is under cultivation and the fields separated by hedgerows, the villages more colourful, red-tiled roofs take the place of the sombre grey slates, and a mellowed atmosphere pervades the cottages and farm buildings.

And so we pass through Thirsk with its cobbled and often congested market place, and on to Sutton-under-Whitestone Cliffe—was there ever a village with a lengthier or more descriptive name? One wonders how the good folk of this delightful village cope with all the printed forms that are sent out requesting us to fill in "Address in full (block capitals)"! How much more simple life must be at the nearby villages of Bagby and Balk or Wass! But Sutton-under-Whitestone Cliffe at least tells us that we are approaching the foot of the Hambletons and the notorious Sutton Bank, now notorious only in memory as we look back on those far-off days when motor-cars were in their infancy and the only means of ascending the Bank was by toiling laboriously on foot or pushing a bicycle or walking beside a horse-drown vehicle. There was no escaping the physical effort, made worse by the roughness of the road. What a relief to reach the top and rest on the edge of the scar and gaze down on the fertile farmlands below stretching away into the far distance.

The edge of the Hambletons as seen from a glider climbing away from Sutton Bank. The flat-topped Roulston Scar is conspicuous on the left (W. R. Mitchell).

Here on top another highway once existed—a highway of considerable importance in ancient times, possibly used by the early Britons but certainly by the Scots in their Border raids from the north, and the drovers bringing their horses and cattle and geese to the English market towns. Much of this highway is now reduced to a rough track, surmounting Black Hambleton, through heather and bracken—wonderful tramping country—but in more recent times certain stretches have been taken over by the Forestry Commission and re-surfaced to facilitate transport needs.

From the Hambleton highway, lesser roads and tracks drop down to the villages tucked away comfortably below in the sheltered and sunny side of the hills—Kilburn and Oldstead and Wass—friendly little villages that have not succumbed to the rash of modern "development" and still retain the spirit of a peaceful English countryside. Kilburn is remembered as the home of the "Mouseman", the late Robert Thompson, who built up a village industry of the highest order, designing and producing with the greatest skill the beautiful furniture with its familiar mouse emblem. A visit to the workshops and showrooms leaves one with the lasting impression that here is a revival of craftsmanship at its best, recalling the work of the Yorkshire-born Chippendale 200 years earlier.

Turning off from Kilburn, a narrow road leads to Oldstead, a typical byway winding along at the foot of the White Horse, cut out of the Hambleton hillside above. This is a landmark seen from many miles away and its size can be gauged from the assertion that a

74

dozen or more people can comfortably be seated on the round of turf which forms the horse's eye! At one time—and well within living memory—Oldstead had its own little industry in the form of a mill, powered by a water-wheel, but although the mill is now derelict, it is not difficult to imagine what a centre of activity this would be in the days when corn was ground locally.

Continuing along the winding lane, close under the hillside where in spring-time the primroses flower in profusion, Byland Abbey soon comes into view, framed in a ruined archway as we draw closer. It is a magnificent ruin which seems to have absorbed the sunshine of centuries, reflecting the skill of the craftsmen who built it. And so on to Wass, a mellowed village brightened by the light stone walls of its cottages and gay, well-kept gardens, the kind of place folk dream about when working in big cities and where an atmosphere of kindness and contentment prevails. Rising steeply from the village a secondary highway climbs up through a wooded ravine to the moors on top, once a wilderness of heather and bilberry but now covered with conifers. It joins the main Hambleton highway through Helmsley and eastwards to the sea. Looking back one glimpses again the wide expanse of the great plain of York and in the far distance, on a clear day, the capital city itself.

Yorkshire is a county of infinite variety—hill and dale, moorland and meadow, forest and farmland—grand country all of it; Hambleton has it all—and in generous measure.

SOLUTION TO CROSSWORD

ACROSS

1. North Riding, 7. Welbury, 9. Nadir, 12. Bay, 14. Pennine, 17. Northallerton, 19. Collate, 20. Sea, 22. Dales, 24. Antwerp, 25. Wensleydale.

DOWN

2. Otley, 3. Ray, 4. Don, 5. Nudge, 6. Swab, 8. Rievaulx, 10. Ripon, 11. Ingleton, 13. Ado, 15. Norm, 16. Otto, 17. Nomad, 18. One, 19. Colne, 20. Steel, 21. Asps, 23. SOS, 24. Age.

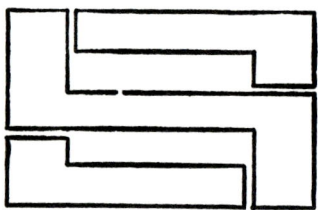

Nimbus the Bull

F. W. White
(illustrated by the author)

Nimbus first charged at Yorkshire readers in a series of separate articles in The Dalesman. *His exploits are reprinted collectively by popular request.*

I DON'T think Nimbus had ever been out of the yard since the day he was born. And that was a good few years ago. He was a great big fellow now and quiet enough when kept to his routine. He could put an evil glint in his eye if he had a mind to and he took a delight in making such a to-do in his box as to get you out of bed in the night. But I never knew him make more damage than an odd splintered rail and once he broke the water pipe to his drinking bowl. He never went for a man, which is more than I can say for the others. No, Nimbus was all right if you let him alone. I'd say he was the quietest of the lot considering his age. I suppose that's why the gov'nor picked on him. It's no more than twenty minutes walk to Newbank farm if you cut across the back pasture and below the edge of the wood. It's a well worn track, for one of us has to go over every other Sunday to do relief when Tom has his weekend off. But it's not a path you could lead a bull along. At least not an eight year old Jersey that has never even seen the other side of the drift house gate. So he had to travel by road, which is a good three miles and passes by the Plough and the bakers. It's nothing new to us to be taking a beast by road. Almost every month we are moving stuff up to the sales. With nearly 200 head milking between the two farms we have a fair take-off. It seems funny to think of it now, but up till the time we moved old Nimbus I'd never shipped a bull in the twelve years I'd been at Gale End. Perhaps you might say the whole thing was lack of experience.

The day we moved Nimbus we had the car and trailer laid on straight after breakfast. Jim had got it nicely backed up to the drift house gate and there was a whole turn out to see the fun. We'd had him tied up since his early morning feed so's he'd get used to the feel of the rope. He was used to the slip chain and sometimes the pole, but a rope across his face and behind his ears was something new for him. He didn't seem to mind too much, but all the same I put a sack across his eyes till we got him in. Of course he made a bit of a shy when his weight tipped the tail-board as he stepped on it, but even heifers do that. It is a bit of a surprise to any beast when the whole thing rocks and clatters on the drawbar hitch. The trailer was none too big for him and he could no more than raise his head a couple of neck creases without scraping the roof and it took four of us to shut the tail board up against his back side. Well, he stood quiet enough inside so I tied him slack to the side and off we set. If I'd been on my own I might say that perhaps I'd been mistaken, but there was Jim with me all the way, for he was driving. He'll tell you the same; that bull never made so much as a shudder. It was as though we didn't have anything in the trailer at all. It was so rum

that just before we turned into the main road I said to Jim we'd better have a look. There are slatted sides to that trailer so I could see inside a bit without taking the tailboard down. He seemed to be all right, not making a muff, still tied up and rolling his old eyes round at me like he always does. Then it just struck me and I said to Jim how I thought he seemed to be a mite lower down than he should be. I thought maybe he'd got down on his knees. Well, it seemed a bit of a puzzle but he looked happy enough and I reckoned we'd better move on. Of course, Jim is always thinking of the mechanical side and he got down to look at the brake cables or something while I was getting back into the car. Then he let out such a yip and yelled come and look quick. He was on his belly on the road staring under the trailer so I got down and had a look too. "Look at them feet," said Jim.

There they were, four of them all right. They were Nimbus's there was no mistake about that. All were planted firmly on the ground. I said to Jim, "That's why he's standing so low." Jim replied, "I wonder how far he's been running." We undid the tail-board to get a closer look. There was hardly a scrap of that trailer floor left— just a few splinters at either end, and old Nimbus standing astride the axle. There wasn't a mark on him though. It must have given way steadily and he must have treaded it off as it hit the ground. He was blowing a bit, I could see now, but it's a mile to the turn off and Jim doesn't drive too slowly. Jim said we'd have to make a plan of action. He's always using these kind of sayings because he was in the Army. I said we'd better get down to doing something as Nimbus wasn't used to being planned about. If he wasn't made a bit more comfortable presently he might take it into his head to bash up the whole trailer. The first thing that struck me was that we dare not let the old devil out. There would be no telling what he would do and neither Jim nor me would stand any chance of holding him. At the same time we couldn't carry on as we were, even though he didn't seem to have managed too badly at galloping along inside the trailer. So it seemed we'd have to mend it.

It didn't take long to find some materials, for Mrs. Jones was standing at her gate watching us and she hollered out to ask what was to do. Mrs. Jones is a very practical kind of a woman and she soon came along to have a look. She said that we'd want a new trailer floor allright and then she slipped off without a word and came bustling back with her old man's foot rule. "Here, get in and measure it," she says and gave me the ruler. Nimbus and me have known each other for a long time. I can't say that being stuck in a trailer too small for him and with the bottom gone out of it, was the best sort of time to be groping around him and trying to measure things. Jim had to stand in front and hold his ring through the slats and keep giving it a tweak every now and then to take his mind off me because he was trying to get a poke at me all the time. I told Mrs. Jones that as far as I could see it was about six and a half feet by three and a half. She took this very brightly and said that's just about what she'd reckoned. Would I give her a hand to take off the privvy door? She had a screwdriver and a jemmy ready and said it wouldn't matter a damn to take off the privvy door because it belonged to the guv'nor anyway and it wasn't as if it faced the road. We took it off like she said. The latch came off, too, and I handed it to Mrs. Jones. She might want it for another door. It wasn't quite the fit it ought to have been but it was near enough.

There was a good bit of fuss to get it into the trailer under Nimbus's feet. If you've ever tried to slide a privvy door under a bull you'll know what I mean. By the time we moved off again he'd got to the growling stage and when a Jersey starts to growl he's looking for trouble. I unloaded him at Newbank with a mask and two side-lines to be sure. He's been at Newbank six months now and we shall soon be seeing some calves out of the Island heifers. They should be a bonny lot with that black face of his. The gov'nor has made no mention of when he'll be brought back to Gale End. Maybe he's thinking the same as me. Maybe Nimbus will end his days there. If ever we come to sell that trailer, whoever buys it will never be able to make out why the floor has got a neet little window in it!

*   *   *

AFTER we'd moved Nimbus down to Newbank farm I had very little to do with him except, maybe, just to feed him and clean him out when I went over to help on Tom's weekends off. They had him in a fine new pen there. It was like something at a zoo—all bars and rails and plenty of room. A sort of yard stood alongside the pen, and here Nimbus could walk about and growl at anybody who passed by. He could also keep an eye on the heifers when he was in the yard, and it was his favourite place, except at feeding times when he'd come inside and rattle his yoke chains and clatter the door so that you didn't forget him. In the walls of the yard were a couple of slits, to be used if Nimbus came for you. The fellow who built the wall must have been pretty skinny, and I think I would have needed Nimbus to give me a hook in the pants to help me through. The gate to the inside pen faced the main yard and it was made like a buck-rake on end and strong as a plough. It had a clever little weighted catch which automatically locked itself when the gate swung to. Tom used to say it was a very handy thing when putting in a restless bull; just a slight touch on the gate and you had him—no fumbling with bolts while he shoved at the other side. Aye, it was a grand place to keep a bull and I think Nimbus liked it a lot better than his old box at Gale End. Then Tom went sick. At least, not the pale-faced and belly-ache kind of being sick, but unfit for work shall we say. It was really an industrial accident I suppose. He'd been easing the milking machine cups on to one of the new heifers when he slipped in his gum boots. It only needed her to put her dainty Jersey foot on his knee cap and that was Tom out of the running for a week or so.

That's how I came to be down at Newbank. Gale End is the main milking unit and Newbank is mostly a mixed rearing farm. One thing they have there is hens. Lots of them. All sitting in rows of little cages in a big wooden house. Tom says there are two thousand of them in there. It looked like two million to me and by the time I'd been up and down the rows a time or two I was dizzy. It was very dark inside too. There were no windows—only some red bulbs and fans in the roof buzzing like a hive of bees. Tom says they lay better that way. The day I'm telling you about, young Jack had just been to feed the hens and collect the eggs before we let the cows in for milking. As we crossed the yard we passed Nimbus's pen and he came up to the gate to tell us it was time for his feed. We stopped to look at

him. He's a fine sight is the old boy as he rolls along under his big neck muscles. Then I spotted it. The clever little catch was swinging clear instead of being fast behind its link on the post. Jack, I says, do you think you could reach that gate before *he* does. Jack got my meaning at once and shot off across the yard for the pen. I think they both got there about the same time and I don't think Nimbus was really competing in the race. He didn't shove or push. Jack meant food to Nimbus, and all he did was to put his great head over the top of the gate and lean on it. Jack leaned on it too from his side and his fingers scrabbled about to find the clever little catch, but Nimbus swung outwards and there was Nimbus standing in the yard twitching his ears. I told Jack to be quick and go and let the cows in while I shut the road gate. If we kept him off the road he couldn't get far, and once the cows appeared he'd follow them inside so's we could get a rope on him.

I got back in the yard just as Jack did with the cows pattering at his heels. There was no sign of Nimbus. Jack said he didn't know where he'd gone, so we shut the cows in the yard and set off to look for him. Mind how you go, lad, I says to Jack; he's probably a bit lively. A big Jersey bull on the loose is no plaything. We paused at the open gate at the other end of the yard. Jack said he must have gone that way and was probably high-tailing it down the other end of the farm. So we set off in the field keeping close to the hedge. Then we stopped and looked at each other. We had both heard it—a great crash and a horrible squawking noise, then a thumping sound and more squawks. We rushed around to the hen house and peered inside. It takes a minute or two to get used to the gloom of the red lights and there was so much dust and feathers about that it was a job to see. But we could hear him all right, somewhere inside, moaning and grunting and knocking the stuffing out of those all little hens in prison. It's them red lights, said Jack, that's what's done it. I said it was more likely to be him leaving the hen house door open that was to blame. I expect he'd gone in for the smell of feed and tried to turn round in one of the passages. Go and fetch his ropes, I said, and get a sack to chuck over his head. We found him about half way along. He had his big backside shoved up against one row of birds and his horns stuck under the other row. He was on his knees and every time he raised his neck the whole stack eased open and a few hens escaped from their cages. There were about a dozen flying around like budgies and two were sitting on his back. Jack said we'd have to raise the Civil Defence to get him out.

Once we'd got the sack over his eyes he was a lot quieter. Getting him loosed from the cages wasn't too difficult although Jack got his hand torn on the wire. We had to back the bull out as there wasn't room to turn him round, and every time his flank touched the cages he lashed out with his back leg and gave the hens a rare old time. They were bobbing about in their cages like jumping beans. Well, the clever little catch got its come-uppance and Nimbus's pen is fastened with a good old fashioned hasp and staple now. I asked Tom the other day how the hens were recovering and whether they'd all gone off lay for ever. "Lay?" he said. "They've been twice the hens they were since. I reckon that bit of excitement did them more good than anything. I always said they must be tired of just sitting and looking at one another's silly faces. That lot must have been as good for them as being entertained wi' television."

* * *

"HOW is he this morning?" says the guvnor, stopping me as I crossed the yard. "About the same," says I, "you'll have to send for O'Reily." "I've just telephoned for him. He'll be along in about an hour," says the guvnor. I went back to Nimbus who was in the big loose box. The fact that he was in there at all showed how poorly he was. Why, he'd bust his way out of there inside ten seconds normally, but now he lay quietly in the deep straw breathing wheezily with a blanket over him. I knelt beside his great head. The shine was gone from those big eyes and his ears drooped like an old nanny goat's. His nose was dry and rough, and the remains of the last lot of honey and gruel I'd got down him were still stuck to his muzzle; too weary even to stick out his black, curling tongue to clear them. I'd never seen a bull so low. We'd had the old fellow ill once or twice before but this time he had me worried. His temperature was awful high for a Jersey bull of his age to put up with for long. Most of the other lads found time during their morning's work to come and look in over the top of the loose box door and see how he was getting on. It was like having a member of the family ill. Presently there was a rumble which told me O'Reily had arrived. He's a good vet., is O'Reily. The guvnor says he's quite a character and they are good friends. O'Reily must be more than seventy now and has some old-fashioned ways about him. His motor car is as old as I am and still has its glass panel between the front and the back seats. O'Reily has a very old and smelly bulldog that always sits on the seat next to him in front. The old bulldog is so horrible that people ask O'Reily why he doesn't put him in the back, but O'Reily replies that he aint going to be chauffeur to no damned dog.

O'Reily always wears a grey suit and a grey bowler hat which goes funny with his red beard. Tom says you could spot O'Reily with one eye if he was hidden in a football crowd on a foggy day. One thing's sure—there couldn't be another like him anywhere. "So here he is," bellows O'Reily pushing his beard over the top of the door and peering at me with his wild eyes. "Lord, how I hate Jersey bulls," he says, "And the worst Jersey bull is a sick one. Devil of a job to get

FWW

'em right. Sooner see to an old donkey any day." Nimbus took as much notice of all this as if he'd been blind and deaf and dead for a week. "He's in pretty poor shape, Mr. O'Reily," I says to him. "That I can see," says O'Reily pushing his way in and giving the old bull a nudge with his foot. Nimbus groaned and lay his big nose along the ground like a tired Labrador. "Can't you get him up?" says O'Reily, "I can't look at him so well all in a heap like this." "I don't think he can stand up, Mr. O'Reily," I says, "he's too weak now." O'Reily did what he could to try and make the old bull rise. He tweaked his tail and flicked his ears, made sharp little yelping noises and flapped with his hat. But Nimbus paid no heed. He just grunted and sighed and lay quite still. O'Reily was feeling in his pocket for his penny. He always got out his penny when there was a problem. His penny is smooth and shiny from all the years of being used. O'Reily was brought up at the Hall where his father was in service and he still lives in the world of stables and horses and grooms. And if he now can't pick up the feet and examine them like he used to do with the horses, at least he can knock on the cattle's chest with his penny as though they were horses to see if their wind is right.

Now it's one thing to knock on a bull's chest with a penny when he's standing up nicely but quite another when he's lying in a heap, and even another still when you're as fat as O'Reily and over seventy. He put his grey bowler down and knelt with care in the straw. Then he lifted Nimbus's blanket and disappeared under it like a photographer. He puffed and shuffled a bit and presently I could hear him tapping on the old bull's ribs with his penny. I don't know whether it was the banging on his bones with the copper or the sight of O'Reily's backside heaving about under the blanket which upset Nimbus. Either way, he didn't like it. Like greased lightning he was up, his head was down and he up-ended O'Reily as neat as you ever saw. "The hell with your bull!" yelled O'Reily clutching at his torn trousers. I got to Nimbus's head and held him steady with his ring. It was lucky he was too weak to do any more or we would have been in a pickle. It didn't take O'Reily long after that to give Nimbus an injection of some antibiotic and get back to his car. He had to cross the yard with his grey bowler clapped to his bottom and he was so angry I was afraid lest he'd have a seizure.

A couple of weeks later I was walking Nimbus in the sunshine when the guvnor came across. As he came up, the bull made a swing at him and rolled his eyes. "Looks like he's nearly recovered to normal," he says, stepping back quickly. "By the way I've just had O'Reily's bill. I must say these modern drugs are getting very expensive. Do you know that one injection cost seven guineas." I looked at Nimbus, who was side-stepping and tugging on his chain trying to get a lunge at me. "Seems more like the price of a pair of trousers to me," I says, leading him off back to his pen.

Some Recent Books

"Dalesman"

IF Yorkshire folk are ignorant of their own countryside it is not for want of being told. The flow of literature concerning the landscape and the towns and villages in it, on the people who live and work there, on the ways they earn their bread, on their customs and habits, on how to discover more about its past, present, and future, is ever growing. More important, the quality of this flow of information has vastly improved. Sentimental verbiage has been replaced by real research and intelligent commentary. The pen is used as a pointer indicating where treasure is to be found rather than as a means of becoming lyrical about it.

We can make a good start with Garry Hogg's *Exploring Britain* in the Shell Book series (John Baker £1-85) for this takes a bird's eye (or motorist's eye) view of almost the whole of Britain from the Scottish Lowlands to the West Country, with a few notable exceptions. It does not cover the Yorkshire coast, nor the Lake District, and only glances at North Wales. But as a handbook for motorists who want to discover interesting and lesser-known territory not too far from the beaten track it will be valuable and informative, and has a plenitude of pictures and maps.

Another book for the motoring explorer is J. H. B. Peel's *Along the Roman Roads of Britain* (Cassell £2-75), which makes plain that although the pioneer road-makers had a utilitarian purpose they certainly opened up some attractive country, more to be appreciated by the car traveller than the charioteer. The author has an observant eye and an informed mind. From the same pen comes *Country Talk* (Robert Hale £1-80) in which Mr. Peel, still motoring but now off beaten tracks, sets down a year's discoveries in 20,000 miles of travelling all over Britain.

North-Country Checklist

David & Charles publish a wide range of titles on the North-Country, a checklist of which is given below. For fuller details of these and other titles in the D & C list, send a postcard for our free autumn catalogue, or send 15p for a copy of our unique annual catalogue (just out) which gives a complete inventory of the contents of over 700 titles published up to and including August 1971.

Baines's Lancashire, 2 Vols., **Baines's Yorkshire,** 2 Vols., £3.15 each. (*David & Charles Reprints*)

Canals of North-West England, 2 Vols., Charles Hadfield and Gordon Biddle, £2.50 each. (*Canals of the British Isles series*)

Climber in Lakeland, Frank Monkhouse and Joe Williams, (January), abt £3, (*Climbing and Walking series*)

General View of the Agriculture of the County of Lancaster 1795, John Holt, £4.20, (*David & Charles Reprints*)

Industrial Archaeology of the Lake Counties, J E Marshall and M Davies-Shiel, £2.50; **Lancashire,** Owen Ashmore, £2.50. (*Industrial Archaeology of the British Isles series*)

Industrial Britain: The Humberside Region, Peter Lewis and Philip N Jones; **The North-East,** John W House; **The North-West,** David M Smith, £4.75 each.

The Lake District at Work: Past and Present, J D Marshall and M Davies-Shiel, £2.75. (*Industrial History in Pictures series*)

The Lancashire & Yorkshire Railway, John Marshall, Vol. I, £2.75; Vol. II £3.15. (*Railway History series*)

The North British Railway, Vol. I, John Thomas, £2.75. (*Railway History series*)

North Eastern Locomotive Sheds, K Hoole, £2.75.

Old Lakeland: Some Cumbrian Social History, J D Marshall, (November), £2.95. (*Old . . . series*)

Old Liverpool, Eric Midwinter, £2.50. (*Old . . . series*)

Old Yorkshire Dales, Arthur Raistrick, £2.25. (*Old . . . series*)

Railway History in Pictures: North-East, K Hoole, £2.10; **North-West,** John Clarke and Allan Patmore, £2.10. (*Railway History in Pictures series*)

The Railways of Consett and North-West Durham, G Whittle, £3.45. (*Railway History series*)

The Railways of Wharfedale, Peter E Baughan, £3. (*Railway History series*)

The Trials of the Lancashire Witches: A Study of Seventeenth Century Witchcraft, Edgar Peel and Pat Southern, £1.75.

View North: A Long Look at Northern England, Frederick Alderson, £2.50.

White's 1853 Leeds and the Clothing Districts of Yorkshire, William White, £5.25, (*David & Charles Reprints*)

The Yorkshire Ouse: The History of River Navigation, Baron F Duckham, £2.50. (*Inland Waterway History*)

See what the North Country looked like in Victorian days! Our reprint of the **First Edition of the One Inch Ordnance Survey** covers the whole of England and Wales in 97 sheets, price 75p each, flat or folded £55 the set. Special prospectus with key to the David & Charles numbering sequence, is available free on request.

DAVID & CHARLES South Devon House, Newton Abbot, Devon

WHEN YOU BUY A BRENTON *BOOK*

YOU BUY A PART
OF
YORKSHIRE HISTORY

BRENTON PUBLISHING

Duke Street   Settle

Unfortunately a motor-car cannot lean over a bridge or potter down country footpaths, for which reason it is not always the best companion for exploring. You have to get out and look and talk and go a-wandering. Without doubt the more excellent way is to follow the old drove roads, once used for the movement (on the hoof) of cattle and sheep, and also geese and pigs and donkeys to the markets of Britain. Such roads followed valleys, climbed hills, traversed ridges and thus created a network of ways through much of the finest country, particularly in Yorkshire. K. J. Bonser has spent half a lifetime exploring these ways, discovering who used them, and all the lore which grew up around them. It is all set down in his delightful book, *The Drovers* (Macmillan £3·25) with a wealth of fascinating detail and many illustrations.

A more detailed account of a particular area is the official guide to the *Yorkshire Dales National Park* (H.M. Stationery Office 45p). This, like the earlier *North York Moors Guide*, devotes separate chapters to aspects of the area—geology and scenery, archaeology, natural history and farming, and the work of the Park authorities. It makes its own comment that it is not "a conventional holiday-maker's guide," but it can still be an informative companion.

As Yorkshire, like the rest of England, is "fathoms deep in history," one of the best introductions to the explorer who is willing to leave his car and roam the moors is *The Archaeology of Yorkshire* by F. and H. W. Elgee, first published in 1933 and now reprinted (S.R. Publishers Ltd., Wakefield, £3·15). This begins with the Old Stone Age and brings us "up to date" with the Vikings. Moreover, it lists the important discoveries and sites (up to the time of the original publication) in each of the three Ridings. It is a classic volume of county history, and copies of the original are hard to find. *The Viking Legacy* by John Geipel (David and Charles, £4·25) carries the story still further by following the Scandinavian influence on the English language. So many of our place-names as well as our personal names had their origin across the North Sea. Some, like Grimsby, are still with us. Others, like Hawksfleet, have vanished. We still have names like Dring, Scarfe and Kidd in our telephone directories.

Those who missed the original publication of Arthur Raistrick's *Old Yorkshire Dales* will be pleased to know it can now be obtained as a Pan Book (40p), with all its remarkable gathering of information about "the life of the land," its villages, farms, schools, lime kilns and water mills, as well as the ways of life of its yeomen estate managers and parish folk. It has, too, the original excellent illustrations.

Beauty Spots and Others

Someone once said that the Victorians found England a land of beauty and left it a land of beauty spots. In our time even these are often in imminent danger of destruction. Some of these beauty spots are included in Bernard Wood's *Yorkshire Villages* (Robert Hale, £1-80), but mainly because they have a story to tell of famous people from Captain Cook to Winifred Holtby. The beauty is apparent in the author's fine collection of photographs which illustrate the book. Whether Leeds was ever a beauty spot is doubtful; its mind was chiefly on "brass." Whether it will become a beauty spot in the future is even more doubtful. Its mind is now set on becoming the "Motorway City of the Seventies." Brian Thompson tells its story in *Portrait of Leeds* (Robert Hale, £2) with many illustrations.

Few would describe Sheffield as a place of beauty yet "the very spot on which Sheffield stands must originally have been one of the most lovely of the whole of this beautiful district." So say Messrs. Pawson and Brailsford, the authors of the *Illustrated Guide to Sheffield*, first published in 1862 and now reprinted in facsimile (S.R. Publishers Ltd., Wakefield, £2-50). To support their claim the authors quote significant names of thoroughfares, "Bower Spring," "Balm Green" and "Daisy Walk." This can scarcely be blamed wholly upon the Victorians, as Sheffield had its "whittle" (knife) making industry among others in the days of Chaucer. This book is largely in praise of that industry and includes engravings of workshops and machines and old advertisements for makers of beer machines, "self-acting water closets," railway whistles and steam gauges. From the same publishers comes the reprint of a more concise *Story of Sheffield* (£3) written in 1935 by John Derry, a former editor of the "Sheffield Independent" who told his story well.

A pleasantly illustrated account of *York* by Peter Wenham, who is an enthusiast for Yorkshire history (Longman, £1-60), is included as a book for young people which older folk will enjoy. Published in that city's 1900th year, it recounts its romantic history as well as much of the violence and cruelty which went with it; the building of the first Minster; the Court of Pie Powder to settle disputes at Fair time; the "financial wizardry" of George Hudson's railway; and the coming of a modern university. As the late King George V said: "The history of York is the history of England." The author finds the real beauty of York "at night, when the commercial traffic of the day has gone, when the shops are aglow with their neon lighting, when the Minster's great central tower is floodlit." Then "the true glory of York can be appreciated."

A particular village, not far from York, is the subject of a careful and entertaining study entitled *Skelton Village—the Continuing Community*, which emphasises the steady growth of the place from Anglo-Saxon settlement to our own day. It is written by the Rector, the Rev. Henry Stapleton, and Dr. M. J. A. Thompson, and is full of human interest. (Sessions Book Trust, York, 75p.)

Beyond the Boundary

Those who have relished Henry Tegner's books on the wild life of Northumberland will welcome his new volume *The Charm of the Cheviots* (Frank Graham, £2-10) in which he goes a'hunting, a'ghosting, and a'fishing in his favourite territory. Once more we have the informed writing of a naturalist who loves the county in which he has spent half a century, even though he is an enthusiast for fox hunting and beagling. He loves the fox in the wild and has closely studied the brown and blue hares of the region and can describe the roe deer as "a very worthy beast of the chase, as well as a charming animal for the observant wild-life lover to study." Another Northumbrian book, this time about places and people, is Nancy Ridley's *A Northumbrian Remembers* (Robert Hale, £1-80) which looks back at a few of the great gallery of notables from that county—Josephine Butler, the social reformer; Lord Grey of Fallo- den, the statesman bird-lover; "Doctor Syntax," the horse not the man, and others. She looks also into that often forgotten territory of North Cumberland and the travels there of Bonny Prince Charlie.

Further away, but from the pen of a writer who knows and loves our Pennine Way and the Lakeland scene, is a useful handbook to *The Pilgrim's Way*, the 120 mile ancient trackway across the North Downs, by Christopher John Wright (Constable & Co., £1-90), again for the motorist who is prepared to leave his car.

For the bird-lover willing to travel anywhere between the Dee estuary and southern Scotland the best guide is W. R. Mitchell (well known to "Dalesman" readers) who records his journeys all over this region in search of our larger birds such as gannets and puffins, terns and barnacle geese. His successes and failures are all set down with a lively pen in *A Few Million Birds* (Robert Hale, £2-50). His many remarkable photographs add to the excitement of his adventures.

Crafts, Old and New

Why did the West Riding, "a small stretch of country, tucked away in hills, not very conveniently situated as regards ports and railways," become the centre of the cloth trade and achieve world-wide reputa- tion? The story is told in Dr. Phyllis Bentley's *Pennine Weaver* (Northern Publications, Halifax, £1-50), which traces the fascinating evolution of the work of the handloom weaver into the modern clothing industry. Simply, and with many illustrations, the tale unfolds and is brought right up to date with the industry facing modern problems; new man-made fibres, trading difficulties, and increasing competition. All Yorkshire folk should read this book.

Yorkshire figures largely, too, in *The English Country Pottery*, by Peter C. D. Brears (David and Charles, £3-15), which is as it should be for there is evidence that pots were made in these parts many centuries ago, probably at the time the Cistercian monasteries were built. The cover of this book has a coloured photograph of Mr. G. Curtis, of Littlethorpe, near Ripon, at his wheel. He still produces "bigware"—horticultural pots, bread-crocks and rain pipes. The gazetteer in the book lists nearly thirty Yorkshire potteries, making their wares according to their regional tradition. Without being technical, the author sets down all that is important about hand-made earthenware.

Scarcely a craft, but certainly "crafty", was the industry of those who ran shipments of brandy, rum, wines, tea, tobacco and lace, brought from the Isle of Man, into secret ports on the coasts of Scotland and north-west England. There is always a thrill in tales of those who ran these black-market cargoes and this makes *The Solway Smugglers* by Gordon Irving (Dinwiddie & Co., Dumfries, 65p) an exciting paperback. Here are smuggling tales galore, with 24 pages of illustrations and a fascinating pull-out smugglers' map, showing landing spots and secret tracks. It would make an exciting holiday quest to explore these old ways—and perhaps to discover a lost bottle!

Equally disreputable, but still a part of history, was the craft of the Yorkshire Coiners, who clipped and counterfeited in remote farmhouses on the moors between Yorkshire and Lancashire. Murder was committed and there was much other violence until the government took drastic action. John Marsh, a Halifax thriller writer, has used his skill on an almost forgotten chapter of our history, and *Clip a Bright Guinea* (Robert Hale, £2) makes gripping reading based on a fine piece of research.

The building and running of steam trains will soon be a lost skill, if not a craft, although the enthusiasm still stirred by them rivals the interest there once was in stage coaches—and perhaps chariots long ago. David and Charles have produced several books for such enthusiasts. *The Railways of Wharfedale* by Peter E. Baughan (£3) and *Railway History in Pictures*, in two volumes North East by K. Hoole and North West by John Clarke and Allan Patmore (£2-10 each): are some of them, with the story of the old *Lancashire and Yorkshire Railway* in two volumes (Vol. 1, £2-75 and Vol. 2, £3-15).

Yorkshire's part in all this development of craft and industry in the wonderful 19th century—which remains a remarkable era however much we may scoff today—is summed up in the facsimile reprint of a volume first published in 1893 by the London Printing and Engraving Co. under the title *The Century's Progress*, and now available again from Brenton Publishing, Settle (£3). In an introduction Dr. Raistrick says: "For the first time we have a pictorial album of the industrial architecture of the 19th century . . . an essential working document for the local historian as well as for all students of history."